The Ladies of the Baptist Church

The Missouri Cook Book

Proved Recipes

The Ladies of the Baptist Church

The Missouri Cook Book
Proved Recipes

ISBN/EAN: 9783744792523

Printed in Europe, USA, Canada, Australia, Japan

Cover: Foto ©Andreas Hilbeck / pixelio.de

More available books at **www.hansebooks.com**

THE MISSOURI COOK BOOK.

"O woman! enthroned by your visions elate
In temples of learning, and chambers of State,—
Politician, or lawyer, or doctor so wise,
Go bottle your tears and pickle your sighs;
For descend you must to every day life
And enter the ranks of the housekeeper's strife.
You may settle like Darwin, the monkey's sad fate,
You may settle all questions of kingdom or S ate,
But no art of persuasion, witty or wise,
Will settle the coffee or make the bread rise,
No doctrines nor creed since eating began
Were known to regale a right hungry man,
Your doctrines, affinities, destinies dim,—
Even total depravity 's nothing to him,
A judge's decision may turn in a dish,
Or a doctor's prescription be found in a fish.
Great thoughts gleam in gravy, and nations are lost
On billows of soup,—and finally lost.
Then do not rebel, but with good common sense,
Submit to the stomach's omnipotence.
Like the ghost of poor Banquo, you always must meet
That unsettled, old question, ' O what shall we eat ? '
And another close follows—' O what shall we cook ? '
That question is answered in this little book."

THE

MISSOURI

COOK BOOK.

PROVED RECIPES.

COLLECTED AND ARRANGED BY

THE LADIES OF THE BAPTIST CHURCH,

FAYETTE, MO.

ST. LOUIS:
FARRIS, SMITH & CO. PRINT.
,.. OLIVE STREET

PREFACE.

When we first thought of compiling and selling these recipes, the amount that would thus be brought into the Lord's treasury was our paramount object, but as we have studied how to be most helpful to those who will patronize us, our solicitude to give back to them value received, has almost overwhelmed every other idea, for we would bring no reproach upon the cause to which our efforts are dedicated. We claim no originality for our work. Like the bee that sips the sweetness of every flower, we have gathered suggestions wherever we could find them. The recipes we offer have been used by the best house-keepers, in our own and other communities, and we bespeak for them a kindly reception and fair trial.

As the book goes forth to stranger and friend, our work is done. We have brought our loaves and fishes to the Master. May His hand direct the distribution, and bless the offering that we lay down at His feet.

We do most sincerely express our thanks to the many ladies who have contributed their recipes, and also, to the advertisers who have so kindly aided in accomplishing our work.

Mrs. Wm. C. Arline.

Mrs. E. W. Bedford.

SOUPS

Agate, iron, or porcelain kettles should be used for making soups. Meats for soups should be put to cook in cold water, boiled gently, and the required quantity of salt added at first, to extract the juices of the meat, and cause the scum to rise. Allow one quart of water and a teaspoon of salt for each pound of meat. Remove all the scum carefully before the vegetables are added. All grease should be removed before putting in the vegetables. It is well to cook the meat the day before the soup is wanted, that the grease may cool and be removed. It can readily be removed while the soup is hot by adding a little cold water to the liquor.

BLACK SOUP.

Cut the meat from beef shank-bone. Mash the bone and simmer all slowly in two gallons of water. Six hours. Set away to get cold. Next day skim off all the grease that has risen. Put liquor on, with vegetables, two turnips, as much cabbage, one small onion, carrots and tomatoes, well chopped; boil till vegetables are tender, then strain through a colander, add a teaspoonful of powdered cloves, and boil all a few moments. —*Mrs. Jeannette Leonard, Fayette, Mo.*

WHITE SOUP.

Simmer for an hour in three quarts of chicken or veal stock, parsley, onion or celery. Cut in small pieces, with a blade of mace. Strain and thicken with two ounces of flour. Boil two minutes. Add half pint of

9

sweet cream. Season with salt and pepper. When about to boil stir in the well-beaten yolks of three eggs. Serve.—*Mrs. H. Everett, Council Bluffs, Iowa.*

TOMATO SOUP.

One quart fresh milk, one pint tomato juice, three table-spoonfuls melted butter, one tablespoonful flour, two tea-spoonfuls salt, one teaspoonful black pepper, one tea-spoonful soda. Let the milk come to a boil, then add the juice, in which the soda has been well dissolved; stir the flour, salt and pepper in the butter, and also add. Boil a few minutes and pour over crackers, and serve.—*Mrs. Mamie White Chinn, Franklin, Mo.*

TOMATO SOUP.

To one quart of water add the contents of a quart can of tomatoes; boil twenty minutes, then strain through a sieve; add one pint of cream, or rich milk; lump of butter the size of an egg, and tablespoonful of flour, rubbed together. Add this to soup, and boil five min-utes. One-half nutmeg grated in, salt and pepper to taste. Then ready for the table.—*Mrs. H. Everett, Council Bluffs, Iowa.*

TOMATO SOUP.

To one gallon of water use half a chicken; let boil half an hour, then add two large tomatoes, or one cup of canned; one cup of rice. Just before taking up put in a cup of cream and a small lump of butter; salt and pepper to your taste.—*Mrs. T. J. Payne, Fayette, Mo.*

GERMAN FRITTER SOUP.

To one chicken take three quarts of water; boil two hours and a half; take three tablespoonfuls of flour, four eggs, one cup of sweet milk; mix into a thin batter and make into griddle cakes. The cakes should be baked as thin as a leaf; cut in small strips and put into a bowl; season with a little mace and nutmeg; salt and pepper to taste.—*Mrs. Joseph Memmel, Fayette, Mo.*

OYSTER SOUP.

One can of oysters, two tablespoonfuls of butter; strain the liquor from the oysters, add to it the milk ; set it over the fire in a vessel ; set in a pot of boiling water; when it is near boiling add the butter, salt and pepper, then add the oysters and let them stew until they ruffle on the edge. This will be in about five minutes. I like it best with a few crackers broken in it, just before taking it from the fire. Serve just as soon as done. The crowning excellence in oyster soup is to have it cooked just enough.—*Mrs. Elizabeth Major, Fayette, Mo.*

BEEF SOUP.

Secure a good sized soup bone and put it in one gallon of cold water, with a teaspoonful of salt; more water can be added later on if necessary ; skim when needed ; while boiling keep it well covered, and boil slowly for four or five hours. An hour before using add one can of tomatoes, or eight good sized ripe tomatoes, also two or three small potatoes, sliced thin, and one teaspoonful black pepper and one tablespoonful of salt. To one egg, well beaten, add flour enough to make very stiff; roll very thin and let dry for an hour ; then cut in thin strips, and drop in soup fifteen minutes before serving; also one tablespoonful of flour, mixed in a little cold water, and add it the last thing just before taking from the fire.—*Mrs. Margaret Unruh, Fayette, Mo.*

BEEF SOUP.

For one gallon soup pare six or eight good sized potatoes, slice thin and boil tender ; take same number large, ripe tomatoes, one large teacup dried okra, one teaspoonful soda, three-quarters cup sugar, a little rice, if preferred. Boil each in separate vessels, till tender, then all together and boil twenty minutes. A medium sized beef bone will season sufficiently. Add salt to taste. Some think cabbage chopped fine and added an improvement; many do not.—*Miss Jennie Keyser, Fayette, Mo.*

MOCK OYSTER SOUP.

One pint tomatoes, well stewed; one quart boiling water; put in a teaspoonful of soda. When it has done foaming add one quart boiling milk; a piece of butter, size of an egg. Salt and pepper to taste. Pour upon three soda crackers, to suit taste.—*Mrs. Samuel Copp, St. Louis.*

BEEF BOUILLE.

Take the face of the rump and put it on to boil about four hours; after it has been on half an hour skim it well; then add carrots and turnips, cut up fine; roast one onion brown on the coals, stick it with cloves and put it in; add half a tumbler of red wine (port is better,) a little tomato, or other catsup, cayenne, or any other good thing. Before serving take out some of the gravy in a teacup, and cut up a pickled cucumber into slices and pour over the beef.—*Mrs. Samuel Treat, St. Louis.*

GREEN PEA SOUP.

Take one quart of peas, cover with about three quarts of water: season with salt and pepper. When almost done add a teacupful of rich cream. Serve.—*Mrs. T. R. Betts, Fayette, Mo.*

BROWNED FLOUR.

Put a pint of flour in a saucepan: stir constantly with a wooden spoon until it is a dark brown. Put away in a covered jar, and use it in soups or gravies. More of this is required to thicken with than of unbrowned flour.

CARAMEL.

Caramel, for coloring soups, is made by putting a tablespoon of sugar and a pinch of salt in a dry saucepan, over the fire; stir constantly until it is slightly burnt. When very dark brown pour in less than a tea spoon of water; keep stirring and gradually add a cup of water. Be sure the sugar is all dissolved. This gives a rich color and is better than browned flour.

FOR COLORING SOUPS.

For an *amber* color use grated carrot; for *brown* use caramel, or browned flour; for *red* use the pulp and juice of ripe tomatoes; for *white* soup use white vege tables; for thickening use rice, pearl, barley or mac-caroni.

FISH AND OYSTERS

HINTS.

Notice that the body of the fish is firm and the eyes full and the gills red. Almost every kind of fish is either boiled, broiled, or fried. Any small fish of the size of a smelt, or smaller, is better fried than prepared in any other way. Fish, like salmon-trout, are best when baked, and some fine sauce poured over them. A cup of diluted cream, in which is stirred two tablespoonfuls of melted butter and a little chopped parsley makes an excellent sauce for salmon-trout. Before broiling fish rub the gridiron with a piece of fat, to prevent its sticking. Lay the skin side down first. The earthy taste often found in fresh water fish can be removed by soaking in salt and water. Most kinds of salt fish should be soaked in cold water for twenty-four hours; the fleshy side turned down in the water.

TO BOIL FISH.

Fish should be scaled and thoroughly cleaned, well salted and put in a cold place until time to cook. Boil in a fish kettle, with water enough to cover it, or wrap and tie in a cloth, and boil in any cooking vessel; if the fish is large it can be doubled in the cloth; cover with more than two inches of boiling water, adding a teaspoonful of salt and a tablespoonful of vinegar to every pound of fish. A good sized fish will cook in half an hour. Be careful not to break in taking out.

Sauce.—Stir into a pint of milk, boiling, a piece of butter the size of an egg, mixed with flour, and a hard boiled egg, cut up fine: pour this over the fish or serve in a sauce-boat.—*Mrs. S. P. Simpson, St. Louis, 1875.*

BAKED FISH.

Clean and wipe the fish dry ; tie a string round the head and dredge with flour, pepper and salt : bake in a pan, with butter and lard, and baste it often while baking: a good size fish should cook three-quarters of an hour. If desired it can be stuffed with the same dressing used for turkeys, only more highly seasoned.

FRIED FISH.

Clean the fish well ; cut up into pieces about two by four inches ; lay around in a colander, skin down, and sprinkle with salt. Let stand an hour, or half a day, if need be. Have the fat hot in a frying-pan. Roll in corn meal ; fry slowly and cook a long time, till thoroughly done through. If desired it can be then dipped in well beaten egg and rolled in crackers after frying, if preferred.—*Mrs. E. Major.*

BOILED PIKE WITH EGG SAUCE.

Any fish will do ; after it is dressed, lay it in the form of a circle, by putting its tail into its mouth, and take a stitch with a darning needle in its head and tail ,to hold it in place. To two quarts of water put half a cup of vinegar, a teaspoon of whole cloves, same of whole pepper, a bay leaf. Half a lemon sliced is a nice addition, and a tablespoon of salt. Put over in cold water, and boil till the fins fall off easily, then the skin can be easily removed, if desired. Serve with egg sauce, made by adding hard boiled eggs, cut up in small pieces, to a white sauce. Pour the sauce inside the circle of fish. Lay a sprig of parsley on top of one side of the fish, and a few slices of lemon at the side of the platter.

BAKED FISH WITH CREAM SAUCE.

Take a tablespoon of butter and a tablespoon of flour, mix in a saucepan over the fire ; add either milk or water, till a pint has been used ; season with salt and pepper. Take any kind of baked fish, remove the bone

and skin, put in a baking dish, cover with the sauce and
dust with cracker dust. Bake a delicate brown.

BROILED FISH.

To broil a shad, or any other fish, grease the bars of
the broiler well. Put the inside to the fire first. The
backbone can be removed by running a knife along
under it, and the long bones can be loosened and taken
out, one, or more, at a time, with a little knife, after the
backbone is cut away from them. Let brown without
burning, till the flakes separate. Turn the skin part to
the fire long enough to brown. Season either before or
after cutting.

SHELL FISH—CLAMS.

To judge whether clams and oysters are fresh, insert
a knife, and if the shell instantly close firmly on the
knife the oysters are fresh. If it shuts slowly and
faintly, or not at all, they are dying, or dead. When
the shell of raw oysters are found gaping open they are
not good.

FRIED CLAMS.

Take large soft-shell clams, dry them in a cloth, and
dip them first in beaten egg and then powdered cracker
or bread crumbs, and fry in sweet lard or butter, or
both, mixed.

FRIED FROGS.

Scald the hind quarters in boiling water, rub them
with lemon juice and boil for three minutes ; wipe them,
dip them first in cracker dust, then in a mixture of two
beaten eggs in half a cup of milk, seasoned with pepper
and salt; then again in cracker crumbs. When they
are well covered with crumbs, fry in a mixture of hot
lard and butter.

TRASK'S SELECT SHORE MACKEREL.

Take a mackerel, put it in soak over night in a pan of
water, skin side up ; take it out and wipe it dry with a
towel, then fry it in butter, and serve hot. If preferred

broil it, and put on hot butter; or if preferred it can be *boiled* in a pan of water, and then served with drawn butter.

CODFISH AND CREAM.

Freshen the codfish to taste; turn off the water; add milk and butter, and a small quantity of thickening; stir well; break in two eggs, and serve when cooked.

CODFISH BALLS.

Boil and mash potatoes, and keep warm for mixing with the codfish; freshen the codfish, taking care not to freshen too much; add to the codfish double amount of potatoes; put in pork fat for seasoning, and milk enough to soften; roll into balls, and fry in hot pork fat until entirely brown.

FRIED OYSTERS.

Strain off the liquor and dry the oysters well in a towel; beat light the yolks of two eggs; add one half teacup of cream; season with pepper and salt; dip in rolled crackers, then in the egg, and again in the crackers; drop in boiling lard, and fry until a light brown; garnish with slices of lemon.—*Mrs. R. P. Williams, Fayette, Mo.*

BROILED OYSTERS.

Drain select oysters in a colander; dip them one by one into melted butter, to prevent sticking to the gridiron, and place them on a wire gridiron; broil over a clear fire; when nicely browned on both sides, season with salt and pepper, and plenty of butter, and lay them on buttered toast, moistened with a little hot water. Serve very hot or they will not be nice. Oysters cooked in this way and served on broiled beefsteak are nice.

OYSTER CROQUETTES.

Take the hard end of the oyster, leaving the other end in nice shape for a stew or soup; scald them; then chop fine, and then add an equal weight of potatoes, rubbed through a colander; to one pound of this add two ounces of butter, one teaspoonful of salt, half a teaspoonful of pepper, half a teaspoonful of mace, and one half gill of cream; make in small rolls; dip in egg and grated bread; fry in beef lard.

FRICASSEED OYSTERS.

Drain the liquor from a quart of oysters; strain half a pint and put in a porcelain kettle, and when it boils put in the oysters; have a tablespoonful of flour rubbed well into two tablespoonsful of butter; when the oysters begin to swell stir in the butter and flour; cook until the oysters are white and plump, then add a gill of cream, and pepper and salt.

FRIED OYSTERS.

Take large oysters, wash and drain; dip them into flour; put in a hot frying-pan, with plenty of lard and butter; season with salt and pepper; fry brown on both sides. Fried in this way they are similar to broiled oysters.

CHICKEN AND OYSTER PIE.

Parboil a chicken, cut up and place in a pie dish; cover with oysters, and season to taste; add two hard boiled eggs, cut into slices, with piece of butter, size of an egg, in the center; dust the whole with flour, and pour on one half pint of milk; put on a puff paste crust, and bake about three-quarters of an hour in a moderate oven.

SCALLOPED OYSTERS.

Cover the bottom of a baking dish with crackers, rolled, or stale light bread; then a layer of oysters, with butter, pepper, and salt; a layer of crumbs again, and so on until the dish is full. Having the last layer crumbs, pour over the oyster liquor, and if that is not sufficient to moisten well add milk. Bake about three-quarters of an hour.—*Mrs. E. Major, Fayette, Mo.*

STEAMED OYSTERS IN THE SHELL.

Wash well and lay in a steamer. When they are cooked enough the shell will open. They may be turned into hot dishes. or served in the shells; to be seasoned by the consumer.

OYSTER PATTIES.

Line small patty-pans with puff paste, into each pan put six oysters, bits of butter. pepper and salt, sprinkle over a little flour and hard boiled eggs, chopped, (allowing about six eggs for six patties,) cover with an upper crust, notch the edges and bake. Serve either in the pans or remove to a larger platter.

OYSTER A LA POULETTE.

Scald a dozen oysters in their own liquor, salt and remove the oysters, add a tablespoonful of butter, the juice of half a lemon, a gill of cream, and a teaspoonful of flour: beat up the yolk of one egg while the sauce is simmering ; add the egg and simmer the whole, until it thickens. Place the oysters on a hot dish, pour the sauce over them, sprinkle a little chopped parsley on the top and serve.

OYSTER FLAVOR.

A German cook has discovered a way to have oyster flavor all the year round. Take fresh. large, plump oysters, beard them, and place them in a vessel over the fire for a few moments in order to extract the juice, then put them to cool, and chop them fine with powdered biscuit. mace, and finely minced lemon peel ; pound them until they become a paste: make them up into thin cakes, place them on a sheet of paper in a slow oven and let them bake until they become quite hard : pound them directly into powder, and place the powder in a dry tin box. well covered ; keep in a dry place and it will be very much appreciated when the true oyster flavor is imparted to fish, sauce and dishes. This makes a delicous sauce for fresh cod.

❈MEATS❈

DIRECTIONS.

Fresh meats should always be cooked in boiling water, and kept constantly boiling, if not, the meat will soak up the water. If more water is needed be careful that it is boiling water; remove the scum when it first begins to boil; allow twenty minutes for each pound of fresh meat. Salt meat should be boiled in cold water, allowing twenty five minutes to every pound. The more gently meat boils the more tender it is.

ROAST BEEF.

The sirloin and standing rib pieces are the best; have the butcher take out as much of the bone of the latter as possible; skewer it to keep it in shape; sprinkle with salt and pepper; pour a little water into the pan to keep the meat from burning; allow twenty minutes to the pound for rare beef, one half hour when to be well done; when done, put the meet into a platter and keep warm; pour off the drippings, and with the dark remaining prepare your gravy by a few dishes of brown flour, a little water, the whole brought to a boil. Send to the table hot.

ROAST PORK.

Season well and roast slowly at first, allowing fully half an hour to a pound; put some water in the pan, and baste often. Cook thoroughly. Fried cabbage is very nice with pork, also any tart sauce; canned vegetables, or turnips, are nice; celery is always admissible.

20

ROAST LEG OF LAMB.

Roast it in the usual manner. When about done, and a light brown on top, make a dressing in this way : Put into a skillet one large kitchen spoonful of lard ; when hot pour into it this batter : One pint of butter milk, one handful of meal, two handfuls of flour, one egg, half teaspoon of soda, teaspoonful of salt, a little sage, and one small onion. Stir constantly until done. Cut the roast several times across the top, and spread the dressing on over the top and sides ; return to the oven and brown. This is *very nice.—Mrs. Louisa Sebree, Fayette, Mo.*

ROAST LITTLE PIG.

The pig should be three weeks old, well cleaned, and stuffed with a dressing of this proportion : Two large onions, four times the quantity of bread crumbs, three teaspoonfuls of chopped sage, two ounces of butter, half a salt-spoonful of pepper, one salt spoonful of salt, and one egg, or it may be filled with veal force-meat stuffing, if preferred, or, it may be stuffed with hot, mashed potatoes. Sew it together with a strong thread, trussing its fore legs forward and its hind legs backward. Rub the pig with butter, flour, pepper, and salt. Roast it at first before a very slow fire, as it should be thoroughly done ; or, if it is baked, the oven should not be too hot at first. Baste it very often. When done (in about three hours,) place a cob or a potato in its mouth, having put something in at first to keep it open. Serve it with apple-sauce or tomato sauce.—*Mrs. Henderson's Cook Book.*

CHAMPAGNE HAM.

When boiling ham add one quart of strong vinegar, one half hour before taking off. This cuts the grease in the ham and imparts a peculiar, sharp, and pleasant flavor. When done put the ham into the oven to bake : first lay three or four little sticks on the top of the pan, on them put your ham; this allows all the grease to drop down in the pan, and leaves the meat very dry. Bake in a slow, cool oven an hour.—*Mrs. J. Kinney, Franklin. Mo.*

BAKED HAM.

Make a thick paste of flour (not boiled,) and cover the ham with it, bone and all; put in a pan one or two pieces of large wire, or any thing that will keep it an inch from the bottom. Bake in a hot oven. If a small ham, fifteen minutes for each pound; if large, twenty minutes. The ham should be placed in the pan, the skin side down. The paste forms a hard crust around the ham, and the skin comes off with it.—*Mrs. Lucy Boone, Jefferson City, Mo.*

BOILED HAM.

Put the ham to soak over the night. then wash and cleanse well, and put it in to boil, with cold water enough to cover it. Bring to the boiling point and place on the back of the stove to cook slowly until tender, when pierced with a fork; be careful to keep the water at the boiling point; turn the ham over once or twice. A very good rule is to allow twenty minutes to the pound in boiling. When done take up and put into a baking pan, and then dip the hands in cold water and take the skin between the fingers, and peel. When cool, and ready for baking, either rub white sugar into it well and bake until brown, or take one egg and beat it well, then add a little salt and pepper, and cracker crumbs all over the top, and brown.

DRESSING FOR BAKED HAM.

Boil tender, then remove the skin. set in the stove to bake twenty minutes, then spread on a batter of one egg, a tablespoon of sugar, the same of buttermilk, and a little soda, mixed. Set in the stove to brown. Stick cloves over it before putting in the oven.—*M. C. Burton.*

BOILED BEEF TONGUE.

Wash clean, put into pot with water to cover, a pint of salt, and a small pod of red pepper; if the water boils away add more; be careful to keep it covered until done; boil until it can be pierced easily with a fork; take out, and if needed for present use, take off the skin, and set away to cool; if to be kept some days do not peel until wanted for the table. Salt tongue, boil the same way, only leave out the salt; or a nice seasoning is to take a saucepan, with one cup of water, one half cup vinegar, four tablespoons of sugar; cook till liquor is evaporated.

BEEFSTEAK SMOTHERED IN ONIONS.

Slice the onions thin and drop in cold water; put steak in pan, with a little lard. Take out the onions and add to steak. Season with pepper and salt, cover tightly, and put over the fire. When the juice of the onions has dried up, and the meat brown on one side, remove the onions, turn the steak, replace onions, and fry till done, being careful not to burn.

FRIED BEEFSTEAK.

Pound and sprinkle well with flour, season with salt and pepper; lay in a frying-pan, with hot lard or butter. Turn frequently until done.

BROILED BEEFSTEAK.

Lay a thick, tender steak, upon a gridiron well greased with butter, or beef suet, over hot coals; when done on one side have ready the warmed platter, with a little butter on it. Lay the steak, without pressing it, upon the platter, with the cooked side down, so that the juices which have gathered may run in the platter; quickly place it on the gridiron and cook the other side. When done to liking put on the platter again; spread lightly with butter, season with salt and pepper.

and keep where it will keep warm (over boiling steam is best) for a few minutes, but do not let butter become oily. Serve on hot platter. Many prefer to sear on one side, turn immediately, and sear on the other, and finish cooking, turning often : garnish with fried sliced potatoes, or with browned potato balls, the size of a marble, piled at each end of platter.

MUTTON CHOPS.

Place in a dripping-pan, season well, and set in a hot oven. This is the nicest way we have ever cooked mutton chops. The gravy may be thickened, or not, just as you prefer. It is not necessary to turn them.

VEAL CUTLETS.

Fry until pretty well done, then take out and dip into beaten egg, and then in rolled cracker, with salt stirred in, and fry again, turning so as to get a nice brown on each side. Make a gravy of water and a spoonful of flour, in the frying-pan, and pour over. Season, if not salted enough ; tomatoes are nice, served with cutlets.

PORK TENDERLOIN.

Have the spider hot, grease it with a bit of lard, and fry both sides brown, but do not cook them through : cover with boiling water, and stir twenty minutes or a half hour; thicken the gravy, and season with pepper and salt. The meat will taste like chicken, and is every bit as good.

MOCK DUCK.

Prepare a good dressing, such as you like for turkey or duck. Take a round steak, pound it, but not very hard, spread the dressing over it, sprinkle in a little salt, pepper, and a few bits of butter. Lap over the ends, roll the steak up tightly, and tie closely ; spread two large spoonfuls butter over the steak after rolling it up, then wash with a well beaten egg ; put water in a bake-pan, lay in the steak so as not to touch the water, and bake as you would a duck, basting often. A half hour in a brisk oven will bake. Make a brown gravy, and send to table hot.

BAKED HAM.

Slice as for frying, put in hot skillet, cover, put in oven and bake. Will require little more time than to fry.—*Miss Nannie Keyser, Fayette, Mo.*

SAUSAGE.

One hundred pounds of meat, ground fine, two and one-half pounds of salt, ten ounces of black pepper, eight ounces of sage. Mix well. You can use a little red pepper, if you like; one-half dozen nutmegs is a great improvement.—*Mrs. M. Pile, Fayette, Mo.*

BEEF HASH.

Equal quantities of meat, and potatoes, a small onion, slice of breakfast bacon, or lump of butter. Boil an hour. Pour a little cream in a few minutes before taking from the stove. Season, of course, with salt and pepper.—*Mrs. Odon Guitar, Columbia, Mo.*

BAKED HASH.

Chop the meat fine, season with salt and pepper, and a piece of butter size of an egg, a small onion, chopped fine; put in a tin baking pan; a layer of meat and a layer of bread crumbs; pour over the whole a cup of cream, or rich milk; put in the oven, and bake slowly, until a nice brown.—*Nellie Keyser, Fayette, Mo.*

BEEF CROQUETTES.

Use cold roast beef; chop it fine; season with pepper and salt; add one-third the quantity of bread crumbs, and moisten with a little milk. Have your hands floured; rub the meat into balls; dip it into beaten egg, then into fine pulverized crackers, and fry in butter; garnish with parsley. To pulverize the crackers roll them with the rolling-pin on the bread board, and sift them.

SWEET-BREADS.

Veal sweet-breads are best. As they spoil very soon, they should as soon as brought from market be put in cold water and left to soak an hour; then lard them, and put them in boiling water, or stock, and let them boil twenty minutes. They will be white and firm. Remove the skin, and put in a cool place until ready to cook again.

FRIED SWEET-BREADS.

Parboil them, as just explained; cut them in even sized pieces; sprinkle over pepper and salt; egg and bread crumb them, and fry them in hot lard.

VEAL LOAF.

Six Boston crackers, three eggs, one tablespoonful of salt, pepper, and sage, or summer savory; three pounds of veal. The veal must be raw, and chopped fine; mix all well together and pack it hard in a deep tin pan; bake slowly for one hour; a tablespoon of butter improves it. This is a nice relish for tea, and should be sliced thin when cold.

OPOSSUM.

Clean like a pig, scrape, not skin it. Chop the liver fine; mix with bread crumbs, chopped onion, and parsley, with pepper and salt; bind with a beaten egg, and stuff the body with it. Sew up, roast, baste with salt and water. In order to have it crisp, rub it over with a cloth, dipped in its own grease. Serve with the gravy, made of brown flour. Serve it whole on a platter, and put a baked apple in its mouth.—*Judge T. R. Bells, Fayette, Mo.*

RABBIT STEW.

Skin, clean, and cut in small pieces two rabbits. Let them stand in cold salt water for an hour; then put on to cook, in enough cold water to cover them, and boil till tender. Season with salt and pepper, and stir one tablespoon of butter, made smooth, with two tablespoons of flour, into the gravy.

SOUSE.

Having cleaned the pigs' feet perfectly, and removed the skin and bones, chop fine; season with salt, pepper, and a little sage. Mould in a pan. When cold it can be sliced, and vinegar poured over it.

PIGS' FEET.

Boil them until done thoroughly, then split the claws, and fry them in batter; just dipped into the batter. *Batter.*—One-half pint of milk, one egg, little salt, flour enough to make it a little thicker than flapjacks; fry them in hot lard.

BEEFSTEAK BALLS.

One and a half pounds of round steak, chopped fine; two eggs, one tablespoon of flour, two tablespoons of milk; salt and pepper to taste; drop in spider and fry until done.—*Miss Cora Jones, Syracuse, N. Y.*

TO PICKLE ONE HUNDRED POUNDS OF BEEF OR TONGUE.

Sprinkle the bottom of tub, or firkin, with salt. Four pounds of brown sugar, four ounces of saltpetre, four quarts of fine Liverpool salt. Mix well together, and in packing sprinkle evenly over the meat. The dissolving of salt and juice of meat will be sufficient to pickle. Keep the meat closely pressed together with a good weight.—*Mrs. Nellie Gannett, Fayette, Mo.*

TO CURE BACON.

For every three hundred pounds of pork use fourteen pounds of common salt, and one pound each of brown sugar and saltpetre. Rub them into the meat, and let it lie for three weeks, rubbing and turning it occasionally. Then wipe dry, rub again with fine salt, wrap it in a thick cloth, or paper; hang in cool place to dry.

OYSTER SAUCE FOR TURKEY.

Drain through a colander. The liquor s boiled and skimmed; thickened with butter and flour, (one large tablespoon of butter, and a scant one of flour,) add a trifle of mace and chopped parsley, then the oysters, stirring constantly until done.—*Mrs. R. P. Williams, Fayette, Mo.*

MINT SAUCE FOR LAMB.

To one cup of hot vinegar add two tablespoons of sugar, one of butter, and one of chopped peppermint.—*Mrs. J. Kinney, Franklin, Mo.*

MINT SAUCE FOR LAMB.

Vinegar, one half pint: sugar, four tablespoonfuls; chopped mint, six tablespoonfuls. Let it stand two hours, and serve in sauce-boat. *Mrs. R. P. Williams, Fayette, Mo.*

TOMATO SAUCE FOR ROAST BEEF.

Put a pint of tomatoes, three cloves, three all-spice, pepper and salt, one small onion (sliced,) a sprig of parsley, in a stew pan, and after cooking twenty minutes strain through a sieve: put in this a scant tablespoon of butter, rolled in flour; cook five minutes, and serve.—*Mrs. R. P. Williams, Fayette, Mo.*

WHITE, OR SUET PUDDING.

To one cup of chopped suet add three cups of flour; season well with salt and pepper; put this dry into a bag about four inches wide, and eight or ten long, as tight as you can, and sew up the end, and steam for two

28

hours. This is a very nice dish, with turkey or meat.—
Mrs. J. Kinney, Franklin, Mo.

TOMATO SAUCE.

One quart can of tomatoes, or one dozen whole ones,
add two cloves, two sprigs of parsley, one bay leaf, a
few slices of onion, and one cup of stock. Cook together half hour.—*Mrs. L. M. Findley, St. Louis, Mo.*

MUSTARD.

Three teaspoonfuls of mustard, one of salt, and one
half of pepper, two tablespoonfuls of brown sugar;
mix with hot vinegar.—*Mrs. R. P. Williams, Fayette, Mo.*

OYSTER STUFFING FOR BAKED FISH.

One quart of bread crumbs; soak in cold water to
soften; two tablespoons of butter; salt and pepper to
taste; one can of oysters; mix all well together.—*Mrs.
Maria Scholte, Fayette, Mo.*

MUSTARD SAUCE FOR BOILED FRESH SALMON.

Two cups of water, two tablespoons of butter; let
come to a boil. Mix two teaspoons of brown flour in a
little cold water, two tablespoons of prepared mustard,
one half teaspoonful of salt; cook for a few minutes.—
Mrs. Maria Scholte, Fayette, Mo.

CRANBERRY SAUCE.

Put cranberries into a sauce-pan; pour boiling water
over them, and set on the front of the stove. Stir in
half teaspoon of soda. Let stand a few seconds, and
pour off, and add just enough boiling water to cover
well. Let them cook till done, then drain and run
through a colander, and sweeten to taste; the water
they are cooked in will make jelly, by adding same
weight of sugar as water; it will jelly in a few seconds
after the sugar is well dissolved.—*Mrs. Dr. T. J.
Smith, Fayette, Mo.*

CRANBERRY SAUCE.

Add one teacup of cold water to a quart of cranberries, and put them on in a porcelain kettle: after cooking ten minutes add two heaping cups of sugar, and cook about ten minutes longer, stirring constantly from the time they are put on ; pour out into a bowl, and when cool it can be removed as jelly from a mould.—*Mrs. H. A. Norris, Fayette, Mo.*

CRANBERRY SAUCE.

Pour boiling water over cranberries, and let them stand over night. Then to one-half gallon of berries add one pound of sugar ; boil about one-half or three-quarters of an hour.—*Mrs. E. Major, Fayette, Mo.*

❧POULTRY☙

___

DIRECTIONS.

All poultry should be carefully picked, and the hair singed off by holding the bird over a lighted piece of paper. Take care in removing that the gall bag and the gut joining the gizzard are not broken. Open the gizzard, first take out the contents, and detach the gall bladder from the liver. If poultry is brought from market frozen, do not hasten to thaw it out before it is wanted for use; till then put in a cold place, and let it remain frozen. When you thaw it use only cold water. Any frozen poultry, or meat, thawed in warm water, will most certainly spoil. Food of any kind, which has been frozen, requires a much longer time to cook.

ROAST TURKEY.

The secret of having a good roast turkey is to baste it often, and to cook it long enough. First, then, after the turkey is dressed, season it well, sprinkling pepper and salt on the inside: stuff it, and tie it well in shape; sprinkle it well with pepper and salt. It is well to allow a turkey to remain some time stuffed before cooking. Pour a little boiling water into the bottom of the dripping-pan. If it is to be roasted, do not have the oven too hot, right at first, until it gets well heated through, then gradually increase the heat. The excellence of the turkey depends much upon the frequency of basting it. Make a dressing of cold bread crumbs, mixed with one-half pound of butter: use no water in the dressing, and season *well* with pepper and salt. After stuffing the turkey well put some of the dressing in the pan, so as

31

to make a richer gravy. Put in the pan with the turkey the giblets, also, to which add a little more than a pint of water. Oysters may be added to the dressing, if preferred. A turkey weighing fourteen pounds should be cooked *four* hours.—*Mrs. M. Hendrix.*

ROAST TURKEY.

After the turkey is dressed, season it well, sprinkling pepper and salt on the inside. Put the turkey in a large meat pan, almost half full of water. Let cook about two hours, turning occasionally. Then take it from the stove and stuff it with dressing, prepared as above. A little sage is an improvement. Sprinkle well with pepper, salt, and flour. Place it in the oven and cook about two hours. If dinner is to be served at one o'clock, the turkey should be put on to cook at nine o'clock.—*Mrs. Elizabeth Major, Fayette, Mo.*

BAKED CHICKEN.

If the chickens are young boil about twenty minutes. Prepare the dressing the same as for turkey, and bake in the same manner. Slice two hard boiled eggs in the gravy.—*Mrs. M. Bridges, Fayette, Mo.*

FRIED CHICKEN.

Clean, wash, and cut to pieces a couple of spring chickens; soak in salt water more than one hour, wipe dry, season with pepper, and dredge with flour. Then fry in hot lard, until each piece is a nice brown on both sides. Take up, drain, and set aside in a hot, covered dish. Pour into the gravy left in the frying-pan a cup of milk, half cream is better; thicken with heaping spoonful of flour, and tablespoonful of butter; cut pastry, rolled thin in squares, or strips; fry a nice brown, and lay on dish with chicken, and pour gravy over all. Serve.—*Mrs. J. Keyser.*

SMOTHERED CHICKEN.

For smothered chicken, the fowl must be split down the back, washed, and wiped dry. Lay it breast upward in baking pan; pour over it a pint and a half of boiling water, in which has been dissolved a heaping tablespoonful of butter; cover with another pan that fits exactly. Cook slowly for half an hour, then baste plentifully with the butter water in the pan; cover, and leave about twenty minutes. Baste again, and once more in another quarter of an hour. An hour and a quarter is long enough for a young fowl. Baste the last time with a tablespoonful of butter, cover, and leave in the oven about ten minutes longer. It should be of a fine yellow brown all over, not crisped anywhere. Thicken the gravy with a tablespoonful of browned flour, and pour over the chicken. The flour should first be wet with a little cold milk, or water, and rubbed smooth.—*Mrs. Jacob Keyser, Fayette, Mo.*

PRAIRIE CHICKENS—STEAMED OR BAKED.

Stuff them, after cleaning, with a dressing of bread crumbs, and seasoning of pepper and salt, and mixed with melted butter. Sage, onion, or summer savory may be added, if liked. Secure the fowl firmly with a needle and twine. Steam in a steamer until tender; then remove to a dripping-pan; dredge with flour, pepper, and salt, and brown delicately in the oven. Baste with melted butter; garnish with parsley, and lumps of currant jelly. Prairie fowls may be stewed, or broiled, the same as other birds.—*From Mrs. Owens' Cook Book.*

ROAST DUCKS.

Ducks should be cooked, and the dressing the same as chicken or turkey. If the ducks are tender, they will not require more than an hour and a half to roast. The giblets should be chopped fine, and added to the gravy, with a chopped shallet, and a spoonful of browned flour.

QUAILS WITH TOAST.

After dressing, split the quails down the back ; let them soak in salt water half an hour, or more, then put in the meat pan. Season with salt, pepper, and butter ; about a pint of water ; baste often ; toast bread, cut in squares, a light brown ; lay toast on meat dish. Place the quails, after they have cooked, and are browned nicely, on the toast, and pour gravy over all.

CHICKEN PIE.

First cut the chicken up, and stew in a sauce-pan until almost, or quite done ; then have a deep dish, or pan, lined with pastry ; put in a layer of chicken, seasoned with butter, pepper, and salt, then cut strips of pastry, and lay across ; put another layer of chicken, seasoned ; put a cover of pastry, notched, round the edges, and cut a cross in the center.—*Mrs. F. Major, Fayette, Mo.*

CHICKEN OR VEAL CROQUETTES.

Two cups of cold meat, minced very fine, add a cup of hot boiled rice, mix together with a fork ; beat the yolks of two eggs, stir in two tablespoons of soft (not melted) butter to a smooth paste ; then add a teaspoonful of salt, a tablespoonful of Worcestershire sauce, and the beaten whites of the eggs, mix well with the meat and rice, and mould into croquettes. Beat two eggs, and pour over the croquettes, then roll them in cracker dust, seasoned with pepper and salt. Boil until a light brown, in lard, which should be quite hot, and deep enough to cover them. Serve with French peas, heaping the peas in the center of the platter, and arranging the croquettes around the edge.—*Miss Josephine Harrison, Denver, Col.*

QUENNELS OR CROQUETTES.

This recipe can be used for only cold meat, but is nice when made from turkey or chicken, chopped very fine. Pick out all little pieces of bone or gristle. Add one sweet-bread, which has been parboiled, season with nutmeg, cinnamon, red pepper, and salt. Roll out crackers into dust, then work into the mixture until you can mould into rolls; then fry like crullers.—*Mrs. J. Kinney, Franklin, Mo.*

CHICKEN CROQUETTES.

(For one dozen medium sized croquettes.) Boil your chicken tender, and chop it very fine. Add one set of brains, previously boiled in salted water. Two minutes is long enough for the brains to boil, then throw them right in the cold water, and skin them, one-half cup suet, chopped fine, one-half small onion, and two sprigs of parsley, chopped together very fine, juice of half a lemon, mix all together, and add enough cream to shape into croquettes. Be careful not to have it too soft. If you mould them pear shape, add a clove in one end, and a small sprig of parsley in the other. This is done after they are cooked. They must be rolled in eggs or cracker crumbs, and fried in boiling lard. Serve with tomato sauce.—*Mrs. Lizzie Findley, St. Louis, Mo.*

CHICKEN SALAD.

Boil a tender chicken, and when cold separate the meat from the bone. Cut it into little square blocks, or dice; do not mince it. Cut white, tender stalks of celery into a bowl, three-quarters inch length, then stir them well together. Make a dressing of the yolks of two eggs, beaten thoroughly, one level teaspoon salt, one of pepper, two of white sugar, two teaspoons prepared mustard, one tablespoon butter; stir in the mixture four tablespoons best vinegar, put dressing into a stew-pan, set it into a kettle of hot water, and stir constantly, till it thickens: set away, and when cold mix it with the celery and chicken, leaving a portion of the sauce to pour over the top. Stick a little bouquet of celery leaves in the center of the salad; then a row around it.—*Mrs. J. F. Williams, Macon City, Mo.*

CHICKEN SALAD.

Take a pair of fowls, boil them, (saving the water for soup next day.) When entirely cold, remove all the skin and fat, and disjoint them; cut the meat from the bones, in very small pieces. Wash and split two large heads of celery; put the white part into pieces; mix chicken and celery together, and chop fine with hash knife. For the dressing, take eight hard boiled eggs, (I use only the yolks,) add to the eggs a teaspoon of fine salt, teaspoon of pepper, one-half gill made mustard, one and one-half wine-glass French vinegar; skim off the grease from the top of the water in which the chickens have been boiled. Use enough of this to moisten

36

well. We prefer it to olive or sweet oil. Mix all these
ingredients thoroughly, stirring them a long time till
quite smooth. After you pour it on the chicken and
celery mix the whole well together with a silver fork.—
Mrs. Dr. Tom. Smith, Fayette, Mo.

CHICKEN SALAD.

The meat of two cold boiled chickens, the same
bulk of chopped celery, yolks of three hard boiled
eggs, yolks of two raw eggs well beaten, one teaspoonful of salt, one of mustard, two teaspoonfuls of
white sugar, one-fourth teaspoonful black and red pepper, four tablespoonfuls olive oil, one teacup vinegar,
and one of cream, one medium sized Irish potato,
mashed, and put through a sieve. Cut the meat and
celery into dice, about three-eighths of an inch square,
mix them, sprinkle with dry salt, toss up lightly with a
fork, and put in a cool place while you prepare the
dressing. Rub the yolks of the eggs to a powder, add
the pepper, salt, sugar, mustard, and potato, then
the oil, stirring well, and adding only a little at a
time. Next beat the raw eggs into the dressing,
and lastly, the vinegar. Put the dressing in a cool
place until you are ready to use the salad, and then stir
the cream into the dressing, pour over the meat and
celery, mixing thoroughly, and serve at once. Garnish
your salad dish with parsley, lettuce, or celery leaves.
This will make sufficient salad for sixteen persons.—
Mrs. John Shafroth, Denver, Col.

POTATO SALAD.

Take four or five good sized boiled potatoes, mash,
and add one-half teacup of cream, beat until light ; season with salt, pepper, celery seed, and one small onion,
chopped fine. Put one teacup of vinegar in sauce-pan,
and when nearly to boiling point stir two well beaten
eggs. Stir constantly until it thickens, and pour over

the potatoes, beating all well together. Put in salad dish, and around the edge lay celery leaves, or parsley. —*Mrs. W. C. Arline, Fayette, Mo.*

POTATO SALAD.

Boil in salt water three large potatoes, until thoroughly done. Beat lightly four eggs, add one cup of vinegar, one tablespoonful of sugar, one teaspoonful mustard, one celery seed. Butter, the size of a walnut; pepper and salt to taste. Put this mixture on the stove, and stir constantly, till it thickens. Then slice the potatoes, and put in layers, with the dressing.—*Mrs. Carrie Morrison, Fayette, Mo.*

SALMON SALAD.

Nine hard boiled eggs, one can of salmon; chop whites of eggs and salmon together, very fine; with a fork cut yolks of eggs smooth, and mix well with oil from salmon, one teaspoon salt, one of pepper, one of mustard, one small cup of vinegar; pour this over the chopped salmon, and mix well.—*Mrs. L. S. Prosser, Fayette, Mo.*

SALMON SALAD.

One can of salmon, fresh; four bunches of celery; chop as for chicken salad; mix with the salmon, and pour the dressing over it. *Dressing.*—Take half a pint of vinegar, and let it get hot, then beat up two eggs, half a tablespoon of flour, half a tablespoonful of sugar, one teaspoonful of mustard, and a little salt and pepper, four tablespoonfuls of melted butter; stir this into the vinegar, and let boil until it thickens, then pour over the salad; garnish with the leaves of celery.—*Mrs. G. Bower, Fayette, Mo.*

OYSTER SALAD.

Pour off the liquor of one can of oysters, chop the oysters fine, add six crackers; roll them with rolling-pin, add chopped pickle and celery seed to taste; then

pour over all a sauce made of two eggs, tablespoon of
mustard, two spoons of butter, a little sugar and salt,
and one-half cup of good vinegar; thicken this over the
fire before adding to the oysters, and best to let it cool.
I think hard boiled eggs, chopped fine, is an improvement. Some use the oyster liquor, and add more crackers, but I like it best without.—*Mrs. M. E. Jackson,
Fayette, Mo.*

OYSTER SALAD.

One can cove oysters, six hard boiled eggs, one cup
chow-chow, or chopped pickle, vinegar, mustard seed,
celery seed; salt and pepper to taste.—*Mrs. Lizzie
Fisher. Fayette, Mo.*

LOBSTER SALAD.

Two lobsters, picked fine, four heads of fresh lettuce,
cut fine; put in a dish in layers, with the lobsters; boil
your eggs, mash the yolks, add three tablespoons of
melted butter, a teaspoon of mustard, cayenne pepper
and salt; two tablespoons of sugar, two cups of vinegar; heat together, and pour over when served.

SUMMER BREAKFAST SALAD.

Prepare two chickens as you would for salad (using
the heart, or liver.) Stir in the above two strained Irish
potatoes, and make a dressing in this way: Take the
yolks of four hard boiled eggs, and the white of one,
(chopped fine.) Rub to a smooth paste, with salt, to
taste, one-fourth teacup of melted butter, a little pepper
and mustard. (A few spices is an improvement.) Put
one-half cup of vinegar in a sauce-pan, and when ready
to boil, stir in two well-beaten eggs, stirring constantly,
until thick. Mix this with the above, thoroughly, pack
in a bowl, and set on ice. When ready to turn out
cover with one sliced lemon, and the juice of one.—*Mrs.
Charlie Smith, Fayette, Mo.*

OYSTERS—A LA CHAMBORD.

One-half head of cabbage, chopped fine : season with salt and pepper, and set in a cool place. Take two whole eggs, or the yolks of three, two tablespoonfuls of sugar, four of vinegar, saltspoon of salt, same of mustard. Put this in a sauce-pan, set it on the fire, stirring constantly, until it thickens ; add a piece of butter, size of a walnut. Let it get perfectly cold before putting on the cabbage. Mix well with a fork, and form in a loaf shape. This can all be prepared several hours before dinner. When ready to serve take large oysters, nicely dried, and breaded, and fry in boiling lard. Have a large platter, very warm. In the center place a thickly folded napkin, and in it place your loaf of slaw, putting on the top of it some fresh sprigs of parsley, and around it hard boiled eggs : cut in dice. And in the dish, all around it, the fried oysters.—*Mrs. J. R. Findley, St. Louis, Mo.*

POMMES—A LA GRATIN.

Have some potatoes boiled in their jackets, when cold, peel and cut in small dice, or marble shape ; put them in a pudding dish. Put a pint of rich milk on the fire ; when at the boiling point, add a tablespoonful of flour, dissolved in a little milk, a pinch of salt, and a cupful of grated cheese. Let all cook about five minutes ; pour this mixture over the potatoes, and bake in oven until brown on top.—*Mrs. J. R. Findley, St. Louis, Mo.*

CHICKEN CHEESE.

Boil two chickens till tender, take out all the bones, and chop the meat fine ; season to taste with salt, pepper, and butter ; pour in enough of the liquor they are boiled in to make it moist. Mould in any shape you choose. When cold turn out, and cut into slices. This is especially nice for lunch.—*Mrs. H. A. Norris, Fayette, Mo.*

A FAVORITE DISH.

One cup of bread crumbs, two cups fresh milk, one cup dry cheese, broken in small pieces, three eggs, well beaten, one tablespoonful of butter; salt and pepper to taste. A very little soda, dissolved in hot water, and stirred in the milk. Soak the crumbs in the milk; beat into these the eggs, the butter, pepper and salt, and then the cheese. Butter a neat baking dish, pour the pudding into it, and bake in a quick oven, until brown. Serve immediately.—*Miss Lizzette Herndon, Fayette, Mo.*

SLAW.

One large head of cabbage, half teacup of sugar, four eggs, well beaten, one teaspoon of mustard, one of celery seed, half teaspoon of turmeric. Mix this all well, then have ready one pint of vinegar, pour it on the seasoning, and let it boil until it is the consistency of cream, then pour hot over cabbage; seasoned with salt and pepper.—*Mrs. Solon Smith, Fayette, Mo.*

HOT SLAW.

Four eggs, one and a half teaspoons of Coleman's mustard, one teaspoon of celery seed, a scant half teaspoonful of turmeric, half cup of white sugar, and a small teacup half full of cream, or a tablespoon of butter, melted; beat the eggs till light, then mix in the other ingredients; then pour in slowly, while stirring a pint of boiling vinegar; then return this to the fire; keep stirring well till it is the consistency of cream. Have the cabbage chopped fine, and seasoned with salt and pepper. When the dressing is done add at once to the cabbage, mix well, and keep closely covered.—*Mrs. Dr. T. J. Smith, Fayette, Mo.*

❋VEGETABLES❧

MASHED POTATOES.

Pare and boil the potatoes; when done, drain off the water; let them stand a minute in the stove to let all the steam escape; add the salt and butter, and mash them free from lumps; add sweet cream, or milk; beat like cake batter, the longer the better, until nice and light; serve in a covered dish.

POTATO CAKES.

Make cold mashed potatoes into flat cakes, flour them, and fry in part lard and part butter, until they are a light brown.

TO BOIL NEW POTATOES.

Scrape the skins from new potatoes, and lay them in cold water for a while, put them into a saucepan, and cover them with water; cover them, and boil for about half an hour; try one, and if done, drain the water off; make a sauce of hot milk, thickened with flour, and seasoned with butter, salt and pepper; pour over the potatoes, and serve hot.

SARATOGA POTATOES.

Pare, and cut into thin slices, on a slaw cutter, four large potatoes (new are best,) let stand in ice cold salt water while breakfast is cooking; take a handful of the potatoes, squeeze the water from them, and dry in a napkin; separate the slices, and drop a handful at a time into a skillet of boiling lard, taking care that they do not strike together, stir with a fork till they are a light brown color, take out with a wire spoon, drain well, and serve in an open dish. They are very nice served cold.

42

TO BAKE POTATOES.

The potatoes must be of equal size. Put them into a hot oven, and bake until tender. It requires about an hour to bake a large potato. Serve immediately; if left to stand they are not good.

FRIED POTATOES.

Peel, and cut the potatoes in thin slices, as nearly the same size as possible; put into a frying pan some lard, or butter, and when quite hot put in the potatoes, fry on both sides until they are a nice brown. When they are crisp, and done, take them up: place them on a cloth before the fire to drain the grease from them, and serve very hot, after sprinkling with salt.

POTATOES BAKED WITH BEEF.

Pare potatoes of equal size, and put them into the oven in the same pan in which the beef is baked. In basting the beef the potatoes should be basted also. Serve them around the beef.

POTATO CROQUETTES.

Season cold mashed potatoes with pepper, salt, and nutmeg. Beat to a cream, and to every cup of potato put a tablespoonful of melted butter. Bind with two or three beaten eggs, and add some minced parsley. Roll into oval balls, dip into beaten egg, then in bread crumbs, and fry in hot lard, or drippings. Pile in a pyramid on a flat dish, and serve.

POTATO PUFFS.

To two cups mashed potatoes put two spoons melted butter; beat until creamy. Then add two well beaten eggs, and a cup of cream, or milk, a little salt; beat well; pour into a baking dish, spread butter over the top, and bake quickly, a delicate brown.

BAKED SWEET POTATOES.

Take large potatoes and put them on to boil, or steam: when nearly done, take out and peel: slice not quite half an inch thick. Put in a baking pan, with a very little water; sprinkle white sugar thickly over them, and spread each slice with butter; set them in the stove to brown. A longer time is required for cooking sweet potatoes than Irish potatoes.

TO BAKE SWEET POTATOES.

Select those that are nearly of a size, not too large; wash them, and put in a hot oven, and bake until done; it requires about an hour to bake a medium sized potato.

BAKED TOMATOES.

Peel the tomatoes by pouring boiling water over them, until the skin will slip, cut out the stem end, set them in a baking pan ; season with salt, pepper, butter size of an egg, and sugar; sprinkle over them a good handful of bread crumbs ; bake slowly for forty-five minutes.

The following recipe is given by Mrs. Martha Jackson, by which tomatoes may be so preserved that they may be sliced and served as fresh tomatoes :

Take the imperfect tomatoes, put in a tin or porcelain kettle, let come to a boil, mash well, run through a colander, then take the juice, place on the fire, put in whole tomatoes, if not too large, if so, cut in half ; let them get entirely heated. put in cans ; seal while hot.

STUFFED TOMATOES.

Select enough large, smooth tomatoes, to fill a baking dish ; cut a piece from the top of each, scoop out the pulp, without breaking the skin ; make a dressing by adding to pulp bits of cold beef, or mutton, chopped fine, bread crumbs, salt, pepper, and onion ; after putting sugar, and small piece of butter in the skins, fill them with this dressing, replace the tops, and bake until done.—*Mrs. R. P. Williams, Fayette, Mo.*

FRICASSEED CHICKEN.

Cut fresh corn from the cob, put in a pot, and just cover with boiling water; let it boil half an hour; mix in a half pint of cream, a tablespoonful of butter, one of sugar, a little salt, and pepper, and let boil a few minutes.

GREEN CORN PUDDING.

One dozen ears of green corn, grated from the cob, or sliced off, then take the knife and scrape the cob for the sweetest part of the corn; beat up well three eggs, add a pint of sweet milk, half cup of butter, one spoonful of sugar, pepper, and salt, stir in the corn, bake in a pudding pan, in a well heated oven.—*Mrs. J. D. Tolson.*

TO BOIL CORN ON THE COB.

The corn is boiled in the husks, which imparts sweetness and flavor, and keeps it moist and tender. The unhusked corn is put into salted boiling water, and when done drain well. Remove the husks before sending to the table.

PEAS.

First boil the pods, which are sweet and full of flavor, in a little water; skim them out, and add the peas, which boil until tender; add then a little butter, cream, pepper, and salt. Time to cook, about half an hour.

CABBAGE TO BOIL.

Cabbage is best boiled, and served with corned beef; otherwise boil a piece of pork with it. Always boil with it a piece of red pepper. Remove the outside damaged leaves, and cut the cabbage into halves, or, if very large, into quarters, so as to better cook the inside stalk; put it into the boiling water, with the corned beef, or pork, and the small red pepper. It will take from half to three-quarters of an hour to be well cooked. Drain the cabbage well, serving it with meat, in the center of the dish.

CABBAGE PUDDING.

Chop cabbage, and boil till tender, in clear water, with salt enough to season; when done drain off the water, put in a pudding dish a layer of bread and cabbage, alternately: season with butter, pepper, and cream, or rich milk; put in oven, and bake to a light brown. This makes a most delicious and delicate dish of cabbage.—*Miss Nannie Keyser, Fayette, Mo.*

TO COOK CABBAGE QUICKLY.

Cut up your cabbage tolerably fine, then put it in real hot lard; then cover with water, and let boil; season with pepper, and salt. Before serving stir in a little bit of soda, and a teaspoon of flour.—*Mrs. W. F. Tieman, Fayette, Mo.*

SOUTHERN CABBAGE.

Scald cabbage in salt water until tender; drain, and just cover with cream; when cream boils, sprinkle a tablespoon of flour; then stir in an egg well beaten, and two or three tablespoons of sugar; add all of the butter you can spare, only allow it to boil an instant after the egg is in, and as you take it from the stove pour in half a teacup of vinegar, more or less, according to strength, and a little pepper.—*Mrs. John Tippett, Keytesville, Mo.*

BOILED CABBAGE.

Pick a nice firm head; chop as for slaw; put in a stew-pan, and pour on boiling water, but do not let the water come to the top of cabbage; put teaspoonful of salt, and cover closely; boil till tender, then drain off all the water, and add one tablespoonful of butter, two of cream, a little pepper; return to the oven, and cook a few moments longer.—*Mrs. H. A. Norris, Fayette, Mo.*

FRIED CABBAGE.

Slice thin, or chop fine; put into a frying-pan, with some salt pork gravy, and a little water; season with salt and pepper; cover closely; cook slowly on top of stove. When done add half cup of vinegar, if liked.

SOUTHERN RICE.

To one teacup of rice put one quart of water, and one spoonful of salt: cook until the grains are done, but not soft, or broken, which will take about twenty minutes; drain off all the water, and set on the back of the stove. Keep it tightly covered, and do not stir at any time, as stirring breaks the grains, and makes it sticky. If properly cooked when turned into the dish, each grain will be whole, and will not stick together; it is much better than when all in a mush.—*Mrs. M. J. Breaker, Fayette. Mo.*

LIMA BEANS.

Boil about an hour; pour the water off; season with salt, pepper, and butter; send to the table hot. Dried Lima beans must be soaked over night, and boiled two hours, or until they are soft, and should have some cream added to the dressing.

BAKED PORK AND BEANS.

Boil with one quart of dry beans a pound of salt pork. Put them on in cold water and boil until beans are tender, but not mashed. Place the beans in a baking dish; lay the pork in the center, on top of beans. Bake in a slow oven till all are nicely browned.

MACARONI.

Bake a quarter of a pound of macaroni until tender. To two well-beaten eggs add a little more than a pint of sweet milk, tablespoonful butter, pepper, salt, a quarter of a pound grated cheese. Pour over the macaroni, and stir all well together. Put into a baking dish, and bake until brown.

SUCCOTASH.

One quart of Lima beans, put on in two quarts of cold water, while boiling cut the corn from a dozen ears, and boil cobs for a few minutes with the beans; when the beans are done stir the corn with the beans, and add one cup of cream, one tablespoonful of butter, one teaspoonful of sugar, salt, and pepper to taste; the corn should cook twenty minutes. A small piece of salt pork, cooked with the beans, is a great improvement.

BOILED BEETS.

Wash, without breaking the skin; put to cook in boiling water; boil till done. Slice and season with butter, salt and pepper. Do not put on the vinegar, as many prefer them without.

TURNIPS.

Peel, and cut in slices; boil with a piece of fresh pork, or beef. When done take out with a wire spoon, mash well, and season with salt, and pepper.

PARSNIPS.

Scrape them clean, cut in slices, lengthwise, and boil with a few slices of salt pork in a stew-pan, or skillet, till tender. Serve in a vegetable dish.

VEGETABLE OYSTER.

Cut into small pieces, and let stand in cold water a short time; boil until done; drain the water off, and pour over milk, or cream. Season with butter, pepper, and salt.

ASPARAGUS.

Get the stalks of equal length; tie up; boil in salted water about half an hour; lay on buttered toast, and pour melted butter and cream over it.

BOILED ONIONS.

When peeling onions keep them under water, and all weeping of the eyes will be avoided. Put to cook in boiling water. Boil a few minutes, then drain off the water, put on more water, and boil again; and still a third, where they may remain till tender. This renders them mild in flavor. When the last water is poured off, add a cup of milk, and seasoning of butter, pepper, and salt. Boil up, and serve. The milk helps to relieve them of their offensiveness. Onions are very healthful, and it would be better for the generality of people if they ate them oftener.—*Mrs. Owens' Cook Book.*

FRIED EGG PLANT.

Pare, and cut in slices half an inch thick; sprinkle a little salt on each side, and press down, for an hour; then rinse in clear water, and dry well with a towel; dip in egg and rolled cracker, and fry a nice brown.

BOILED CARROTS.

Wash and scrape well, and lay in cold water half an hour; if large, split them; boil until tender; butter well, and serve hot.

BOILED HOMINY.

Soak over night in cold water; next day put it into a pot, with at least two quarts of water to a quart of hominy, and boil slowly three or more hours, until soft; drain in a colander, and stir in butter, pepper, and salt. In cold weather a large quantity can be boiled, and used when needed.

TO BOIL STRING BEANS.

Put a piece of salt pork, or bacon, in cold water; when it boils, skim; put in beans, and boil about two hours.

SCALLOPED TOMATOES.

Put in a buttered baking dish a layer of bread, or cracker crumbs, seasoned with bits of butter; then a layer of sliced tomatoes, seasoned with salt, pepper, and sugar, if desired; then a layer of crumbs, and so on till the dish is full, finishing with the crumbs. Bake about three-quarters of an hour.

PARSNIPS. SAUTÉD.

Parboil them, after cutting lengthwise; place in a baking dish, with sugar and butter—a layer of the slices; then the butter and sugar; then slices; so on until the dish is full. Pour in water enough to make a syrup, and bake.—*Miss Lou Smith, Fayette, Mo.*

SALSIFY.

Having scraped the salsify roots, and washed them in cold water, parboil them; then take them out; drain them; cut them into large pieces, and fry them in butter. Salsify is frequently stewed slowly till quite tender, and then served up with melted butter; or it may be first boiled, then grated, and made into cakes, to be fried in butter. Salsify must not be left exposed to the air, or it will turn blackish.

CAULIFLOWER.

Trim off the outside leaves, and put the cauliflower into well salted boiling water. Be careful to take it out as soon as tender, to prevent it dropping into pieces. Make in a saucepan a white sauce, in this way: Put butter the size of an egg into the saucepan, and when it bubbles, stir in a scant half teacupful of flour; stir well until cooked, then add two teacupfuls of thin cream, some pepper and salt; stir it over the fire until perfectly smooth; pour the sauce over the cauliflower, and serve.

OMELETTE.

Five eggs, pint of sweet milk, four tablespoons of flour; season with salt and pepper. Beat the yolks of the eggs until very light, then add pepper and salt. Take from the pint of milk a teacupful, into it stir until smooth the four tablespoons of flour; stir this with the other milk into the eggs, and lastly, the whites beaten to a stiff froth. Have skillet hot, and grease well with lard, or butter; when slightly brown turn one half over the other. Serve on oval-shaped meat dish.—*Mrs. E. Major, Fayette, Mo.*

OMELETTE.

For a small family, take six eggs, beat the yellows and whites separately. Put the eggs together, and beat for a few minutes; add a little salt and pepper, if you like. If you have cold boiled ham at any time, chop some fine, and put it in; it makes the omelette very nice. Cook in a stewpan well greased with butter. —*Mrs. E. W. Bedford.*

OMELETTE.

In the first place, be sure your eggs are fresh, or you will fail. Break them into an earthen dish, and beat just enough to mix the whites and yolks together nicely, then add a tablespoonful of sweet milk, or cream, for every egg, and then beat thoroughly, as you would for sponge cake. Have your pan perfectly dry, and hot enough to melt, but not to brown your butter; turn in your omelette, and place over the fire at once, but be careful it does not burn. Take a thin-bladed knife and run carefully under the bottom, to let what is

51

not cooked get below. Do not cook the whole mass
solid, or you will have it hard and dry, as its own heat
will cook it some time after it is taken up; commence
at one side and carefully roll over and over until the
whole is in a roll. Let it brown a nice brown. Turn
out on a hot dish, and serve. Do not put on a grain of
salt while cooking, or it will be tough and flat. The
butter, if well salted, will make it salt enough.—*Mrs.
L. Cook, Fayette, Mo.*

CHEESE OMELETTE.

Six eggs, one cup of grated cheese, pepper and salt
to taste; beat all together about one minute. Have a
bright, smooth frying-pan; let it heat well, and put in
a piece of fresh butter, size of half an egg; now pour on
your beaten eggs; stir from one side to the other with a
spoon, until they are set. It is then ready to serve.
With a quick movement of the cake lifter, throw one
half over the other, then slide on a warm platter, and
eat while hot.—*Mrs. J. R. Findley, St. Louis, Mo.*

SCRAMBLED EGGS.

Six eggs beaten hard a few minutes; a good pinch of
salt and pepper; a half teacup of rich milk; a tablespoon of melted butter; have your skillet quite hot,
and well greased; pour in the mixture, and begin stirring at once; keep stirring well from the bottom, till it
is well set, which will be in a few seconds, then empty
into a warmed dish, and keep closely covered. It
should be prepared just before going to table.—*Miss
Lou Smith, Fayette, Mo.*

BAKED EGGS.

Put a little butter in pan, when warm, put in the eggs,
(be careful not to break the yolks,) salt and pepper.
Bake in the oven till the whites are hard.—*Mrs. Mumpower, Fayette, Mo.*

POACHED EGGS.

Break the eggs into boiling water, and sprinkle salt over them. When the white is well set, take them out : pour over a little melted butter; season with pepper. Serve on buttered toast, if you prefer.

SCRAMBLED EGGS.

Beat six or eight eggs very light; add a little salt; put them into a warm frying-pan, with butter, or lard ; stir until they are well thickened, but not hard; season with pepper.

TO FRY EGGS.

Melt a piece of butter in a frying pan ; put the eggs in carefully, so as not to break the yolks ; sprinkle with salt, and as soon as the whites are set, serve on a hot dish. The butter should not be allowed to get too hot, and only a couple of eggs should be fried at a time. A small frying-pan should be used.

TO PREPARE EGGS FOR LUNCH.

To boil the eggs, put them in cold water, which will prevent them bursting, as they would if they were put in hot water to boil. When done put them in cold water, so the shell will come off nicely. Cut them in halves, lengthwise; remove the yellows ; mash them up, and season with butter, pepper, salt, celery seed and a little vinegar. Put the yellows back into the whites, and put the halves together. You have a very pretty dish if you will tie around each one a piece of narrow blue ribbon.

OYSTER OMELETTE.

Beat six eggs to a thick cream ; season with pepper and salt; have ready one dozen large oysters ; cut them in half; pour the eggs in a pan, with hot butter in it; drop the oysters over it as carefully as you can ; fry a light brown, and serve hot.

STUFFED EGGS.

Boil the eggs hard; and cut them in two; take out carefully the yolks, which mash well, adding a little finely minced onion, chopped parsley, pepper, and salt. Mash also double the quantity of bread, which has been soaked in milk; mix bread, yolks, etc., together; then bind them with a little raw yolk of egg: taste to see if they are seasoned properly. Stuff the eggs with the mixture, so that each half has the appearance of containing a whole round yolk; smooth the remainder of the mixture on the bottom of a pie pan; arrange the halves symmetrically in this bed; brown a little in the oven.

TO KEEP EGGS.

Put a two inch layer of salt in bottom of stone jar; then a layer of fresh eggs, small end down; then salt, then eggs, and so on till jar is full, with a layer of salt at top; cover and put in a cool place, but not where they will freeze. This is a simple, easy, and inexpensive way, and has been tested for years.

CRACKED WHEAT.

Rinse thoroughly with cold water: two teacups of wheat; add four cups of cold water; place the pan in a pan of water, and cover closely. In half an hour or so stir, and salt to taste. Let it steam four or five hours, stirring once or twice. Nice, hot or cold, for breakfast. Serve with cream.

OATMEAL PORRIDGE.

To three parts of boiling water add one part oatmeal. Cover closely, and cook slowly for half hour. Do not stir it if you would prevent it being sticky. Serve with sugar and cream.

HOMINY.

Wash in two waters one cup of hominy; then stir it into one quart of boiling water, with a little salt, and boil sixty minutes. Be careful that it does not burn.

HOMINY FRITTERS.

One egg, one half cup of sweet milk, one tablespoonful
of flour, one quart of boiled hominy, a pinch of salt;
roll into oval balls, with floured hands; dip in a well-
beaten egg, and then in dried bread crumbs, and fry in
hot lard.

TO COOK HOMINY.

To one quart of hominy use five quarts of water;
cook slowly. When soft, skim out into a crock, and set
it in a cool place. To prepare for the table, to one
quart of cooked hominy use one spoonful of butter,
or lard, that has been heated. Add half teacupful of
cream, or rich milk; salt to taste.

DUTCH CHEESE.

Take a crockful of clabbered milk, and set it on the
stove to heat; when the whey and clabber separate,
put it into a jelly bag, and hang it up where it will
drain dry. Season; serve with cream.

❧BREAD❧

LIGHT BREAD.

One quart of flour; two tablespoons yeast; one small tablespoon lard; one teaspoon salt; mix up with cold water and knead the dough well; when the dough is risen very light, knead the second time, and make into loaves and light rolls, and let rise again. Bake one hour.—*Mrs. Dr. Snelson, St. Joseph, Mo.*

TO MAKE YEAST AND LIGHT BREAD.

Boil two or three small potatoes; mash them; add a pint of flour, and scald it with the water in which the potatoes were boiled; then stir to a stiff batter, and when cool, add more water, until thinner; then add your baker's yeast, or soak a cake of dry yeast and put in a warm place to rise; do not use the yeast as soon as it rises to the top of the bowl, but wait until it falls again, then it is ready for use; one cup of this yeast will be sufficient to make a pan of rolls or a loaf of bread. You can either keep this yeast fresh on ice, or make it into dry yeast-cakes, by adding enough cornmeal to make stiff, cool and cut in square cakes; dry thoroughly, then put in a sack and keep in a dry place. When you want to make light bread, make a sponge over night, of a pint or more flour, with luke-warm water, and add one or two cold potatoes, mashed fine, add either a cup of fresh yeast or a cake of dry yeast, soaked; set in a warm place and let rise. The next morning early, make up your bread; take a quart or more flour, teaspoon of salt, tablespoon of lard, and make a stiff dough with either lukewarm water or sweet

56

milk ; knead well about five minutes and set to rise; as
soon as light, make into loaves and put in pans. Bake
in a hot oven.—*Mrs. W. F. Tieman, Fayette, Mo.*

LIGHT BREAD.

To two quarts of flour, add two tablespoons of
lard, teaspoon of salt, one-half teacup of white sugar,
one coffeecup of yeast; mix with lukewarm water;
knead until smooth. Grease a large earthen bowl well;
put the dough in, then turn it over; the grease on the
top will prevent a crust forming on top; set in a warm
place to rise. To have rolls for tea, make up the bread
early in the morning, and at four o'clock make out the
rolls. (In making out the rolls or loaves, never add
any more flour, it will make the bread tough). Set in
some warm place to rise. In baking, put a pan of
water on the grate to keep them from browning too
quickly on top.

For the yeast, take about three good-sized potatoes;
peel, and boil until done; take out of the water and
mash until smooth; mix small teacup of flour with
potatoes; pour the water in which the potatoes were
boiled into this, and beat until smooth; put over the
fire and cook as you would starch, stirring constantly;
only requires a few minutes to cook. Dissolve a cake
of National yeast in a little cold water, and stir into the
above when cold. This yeast makes better bread a day
or two after it is made.—*Mrs. E. Major, Fayette, Mo.*

SALT-RISING BREAD.

Take one-half teacup of sweet milk; let it come to
boiling heat; then stir in meal to the consistency of
mush; let it stand in a warm place over night, then
make a stiff batter of flour and warm water or milk;
add the meal, a pinch of sugar and salt; let stand in
warm water until it rises; don't have the water too
warm; make your bread of the rising and warm milk

or water and tablespoon of lard and a little salt; I always take the same quantity of milk as rising; work well, and then mold in pans. Don't bake in a very hot oven.—*Mrs. Hampton L. Watts, Fayette, Mo.*

SALT-RISING BREAD.

Over night, take one teacup of milk, and heat to boiling heat; stir in a large tablespoon of cornmeal, set aside till morning, and pour in boiling water until lukewarm, add one teaspoon of sugar and pinch of salt; stir in flour until it makes a thick batter, and set in warm place to rise; take two quarts of flour, and tablespoon of lard, teaspoon of salt, tablespoon of sugar, teacup sweet milk and warm water sufficient to make dough stiff enough to mould into loaves; knead well and set to rise, and bake in a moderately warm oven.— *Mrs. Lankford Cook, Fayette, Mo.*

BOSTON BROWN BREAD.

One cup of sour milk, one cup of cornmeal, one cup of Graham flour, half a cup of molasses, half a teaspoonful of salt, half teaspoon of soda; pour the batter into a covered mold and set in a large vessel of boiling water; place a weight upon the mold to keep it steady, do not allow the water to stop boiling, and in replenishing, take care that the water does not reach the top of the mold; boil three or four hours, then turn the bread out of the mold, and dry it in the oven for ten minutes.—*Josephine Harrison, Denver, Col.*

BROWN BREAD.

One cup of cornmeal, four cups of Graham flour, three cups of sweet milk, one cup of molasses, one teaspoon of soda; put into the molasses, a little salt; steam three hours.—*Mrs. Mary Gay, Fayette, Mo.*

BROWN BREAD.

Three eggs, two cups of milk, one sour and one sweet, (if you haven't the sweet milk, use strong coffee) one cup of Orleans molasses, two cups of Graham flour, one of cornmeal, teaspoon of baking powder, small teaspoon of soda; salt to taste: pour this into two or three quart cans, set in your steamer and steam three hours.—*Mrs. Bettie Tutt Dunaway, Oswego, Kan.*

CINNAMON ROLLS.

Take a part of the dough that you have prepared for rolls, and roll it out till it is the thickness of biscuit: take two tablespoons of cinnamon, one of butter, four of sugar, and stir them well together; then spread on your dough, turn over, and spread the mixture again; then roll the dough together and cut in thin slices: put them in a pan to rise again; bake about half an hour. The same can be done with biscuit dough.—*Mrs. Fannie Everett, Fayette, Mo.*

WAFFLES.

One egg beaten light, one quart of fresh buttermilk, one quart of flour, teaspoon of soda, teaspoon of salt. Beat thoroughly.—*Mrs. Wilson Smith, Fayette, Mo.*

MUFFINS.

Two eggs beaten separately; one quart of flour; not quite a quart of buttermilk, teaspoon of soda, teaspoon of salt; add whites last; beat until light. The batter for muffins should be thicker than for waffles; have irons hot; grease well; bake in quick oven; as soon they rise, put on the top or upper grate to brown.

MUFFINS.

Three cups of flour, three cups of sweet milk, three eggs, butter, half the size of an egg, one teaspoonful of yeastpowder, a little salt. Bake in a quick oven.—*Mrs. H. K. Givens, Fayette, Mo.*

SODA BISCUIT.

One quart of flour, one-half teaspoon of soda and one of salt, mixed in the flour; lump of lard or butter, the size of an egg; one-half pint of clabber or buttermilk; have a soft dough, as soft as can be rolled out, and stick with a fork. Bake in quick oven.—*Mrs. Joseph Tolson, Fayette, Mo.*

SODA BISCUIT.

One quart of flour, one pint of buttermilk, one half teacup of lard, one level teaspoon of soda, one level teaspoon of salt; sift the soda in the flour; mix the lard well with the flour; add the milk, and work until smooth; cut out as rapidly as possible, and bake in a quick oven.—*Mrs. M. J. Breaker, Fayette, Mo.*

YEASTPOWDER BISCUITS.

One quart of flour, two heaping teaspoons of baking-powder, lard, size of an egg, one teaspoon of salt; milk enough to make a soft dough. Mix just before baking, and bake in quick oven.—*Mrs. E. R. Hendrix, Fayette, Mo.*

BEAT BISCUIT.

One pint of flour, teaspoon of salt, a small teacup half full of rich, sweet cream; beat till smooth and light.—*Mrs. Wilson Smith, Fayette, Mo.*

FRENCH BISCUITS.

Two quarts of flour, three eggs, beaten separately; little more than a pint of warm, sweet milk; teacup of sugar, teacup of yeast, large iron spoon of lard, and a little salt. Make into dough, and work well. Let it rise. If you want the biscuit for tea, make up early in the morning, and about four o'clock work again. Roll out *thin*, and cut into biscuits; lard on one side, and lay another on that already greased with lard; let them rise again. Bake in rather a quick oven.

Our cook would often give me the proportions, as I would write this recipe off for friends, and after she had finished, she would say : " *Now* please put down, ' and if you do it *right*, it's no trouble *nuther.*' "—*Mrs. E. Major, Fayette, Mo.*

INDIAN BREAD.

Three cups of rye flour, three cups of Indian meal, two-thirds of a cup of sugar, four and one-half teaspoons of baking powder; salt; with sweet milk, like Johnny-cake. Steam three and one-half hours, and brown in the oven.—*Miss Cora Jones, Syracuse, N. Y.*

RECIPE FOR CORN BREAD.

Take one pint cornmeal, pour in sufficient boiling water to scald it well, let cool, then add a teaspoonful of salt, a piece of lard as large as a walnut, and one or two eggs, and beat thoroughly ; put in a little sweet milk to make it brown nicely ; bake in gem pans, or put in a stove pan, in spoonfuls. Bake in quick oven. —*Mrs. J. R. Estill, Estill, Mo.*

FRITTERS.

Two eggs, one cup of milk, pinch of salt. one and a half cups of flour, with one teaspoon baking powder. Serve with powdered sugar, or maple syrup. Fry in hot lard, as you do crullers.

CORN BATTER BREAD.

One quart of clabber, three eggs, one tablespoon of butter, or lard, one tablespoon of sugar, one half teaspoon of soda. Stir in meal enough to make a thin batter. To make good bread have the batter thin. Have the pan well greased, and hot. Put in the oven and bake one hour.

EGG BREAD.

One egg, beat well; add one pint of buttermilk, one level teaspoon of soda, one of salt. Stir until it foams, then add one pint of meal, and one teaspoon of melted lard. We prefer an iron skillet for egg bread; have hot, and well greased. Bake in hot oven.

CORN BATTER CAKES.

Two eggs, beaten separately, one pint of buttermilk, one level teaspoon of soda, one of salt, one pint of meal, one-half teacup of sweet milk; add the whites last. Have griddle hot, and well greased.

CORN MUFFINS.

Muffins are made by the above recipe by adding a teaspoon of melted lard. Bake in muffin irons, hot, and well greased.

PLAIN CORN BREAD.

With a light quart of meal mix well one teaspoon of soda, one half teaspoon of salt, and one pint of fresh buttermilk. Bake in a moderate oven.

PLAIN CORN BREAD.

One quart of meal, teaspoon of salt. Mix with cold water. Make in small loaves. Have the skillet hot. Sprinkle meal in skillet, to prevent the bread sticking.

SALLY LUNN.

One teacup of yeast, one pint warm sweet milk, a piece of butter size of hen egg, two pints of flour, two eggs, one tablespoon sugar. When ready to put to rise, work in one-half teaspoon of soda.

SALLY LUNN.

Rise the dough as you would for rolls. When it is well risen, do not take it out of the bucket till you add one cup of sugar, three eggs, one half cup of butter; work all together with the hand, till the eggs and sugar are thoroughly mixed, then pour into a warm, greased pan, and rise as you would rolls.

PUFFETS FOR TEA.

Three eggs, one cup sugar, two-thirds of a cup of butter, three pints flour, three teaspoonfuls of baking powder. Bake in muffin rings, and serve warm.—*Mrs. M. Bridges, Fayette, Mo.*

MOONSHINE TOAST.

Take what bread you want to use for toast, and soak it a few minutes in sweet milk. Take it out and put it in a stove pan; cover with milk. It will soon be a nice brown, then take each piece and butter it while it is hot, and lay two together.—*Mrs. T. J. Payne, Fayette, Mo.*

FRENCH TOAST.

Beat two eggs in a dish; put in a half pint of sweet milk, a little pepper, and a pinch of salt; slice some cold light bread; have your skillet hot, with equal parts of lard and butter. Dip the bread in the milk and eggs half a minute; turn over, and fry until a light brown. An excellent way to use stale bread.—*Mrs. John McCrary, Huntsville, Mo.*

BREAD CAKES.

Soak over night, in a little warm water, dry bread enough to make a quart. Drain off the water in the morning. To one cup of flour add a teaspoon of baking powder. Mix well; beat up the soft bread with some milk; add to this two well-beaten eggs, a teaspoonful of salt, then the flour and baking powder, and last of all, a tablespoonful of melted butter. The butter should flow easily from the spoon; rub a bit of salt pork on the griddle, hot, and drop a spoonful of batter for each cake.

BREAKFAST CAKES.

Mix one quart of buckwheat flour, and a little salt, with as much water, warm, as will make a thin batter; beat it well, then add the yeast, and a very little syrup. When well mixed set it in a warm place to rise; as soon as it is very light, add half teaspoonful of soda. Have the griddle hot, and well greased, and bake the cakes to a delicate brown. Pour over them melted butter, and serve hot.—*Mrs. E. Major, Fayette, Mo.*

STRAWBERRY SHORT CAKE.

Make a dough, the same as for soda biscuit; roll it thin, the size of your jelly-cake pans, and when done, open the cakes, and butter both the inside and outside layers; have your strawberries nicely picked, and sugared, before you prepare the dough, in order to have plenty of juice; spread your berries in both the upper and lower layer, putting one layer on top of the other; set it again in the oven for a few minutes, not long, to cook the berries.—*From My Mother's Cook Book.*

❖PUDDINGS❖

GENERAL DIRECTIONS.

If a pudding is to be boiled or steamed, always have the water boiling before the pudding is put in. Do not allow it to stop boiling for an instant while the pudding is cooking. Puddings are boiled in cloths, or in moulds, tied in cloths; they should be tied tightly, and the moulds be buttered before the puddings are put in them. A pudding cloth should be made of thick twilled muslin, and always before using it, wash it out in clean water, and flour it well before pouring in the pudding, allowing room for the pudding to swell. Puddings are much nicer and lighter steamed than boiled. Have the steamer hot before putting in the pudding. All puddings in which berries are used, require more flour than those without; and it must be remembered, fruit (dusted with a little flour) should always be added the last thing. All puddings, of the custard kind, require a very gentle oven. Those made of batter should be put into one sufficiently brisk to raise them quickly, without scorching them. Such as contain suet and fruit, must have a well heated, but not fierce oven. Always be sure and butter the dish well, before the pudding is turned in.

FRUIT PUDDING.

One coffee cup of beef suet, chopped very fine, one coffee-cup of molasses, one of buttermilk, one of raisins, seeded and chopped, one of currants, washed and dried, three of flour, well sifted, one teaspoonful of cinnamon, one half teaspoonful of cloves, also of mace, one grated nutmeg. Mix all well. Pour in a well greased pudding

65

mould, and steam four hours.—*Mrs. Dr. Thomas Smith, Fayette, Mo.*

SUET PUDDING.

One cup of molasses, one of sweet milk, one of chopped suet, two of raisins, three of flour, one teaspoon of soda, a little salt, cloves, cinnamon and nutmeg, to your taste. Boil two and a half hours.—*Mrs. Dr. J. D. Smith, St. Joseph, Mo.*

SUET PUDDING.

One cup of molasses, one of sweet milk, one of suet, chopped fine, one of raisins, one of currants, two and one half cups of flour, one half teaspoon of soda, one half teaspoon of clove, same of allspice, one teaspoon cinnamon, and a half nutmeg. Mix well, and steam two and one-half hours.—*Mrs. W. M. Robertson, Fayette, Mo.*

DOVER PUDDING.

Three coffee cups of flour, one teacup of finely chopped suet, one teacup of milk, two-thirds cup of molasses, one teaspoonful of soda, one cup of chopped raisins, one teaspoonful of cloves, a small nutmeg, and a little salt; first mix two cups of the flour with the suet, add the milk, soda, and molasses, then the third cup of flour; lastly, the raisins. Steam in a mould five hours.—*Mrs. Evelina Carson, Fayette, Mo.*

BOILED RAISIN PUDDING.

Take one pint of sweet milk, five eggs, one teacup of seeded raisins, well floured; enough flour to make a stiff batter; put in a sack, and drop in boiling water. Boil one hour and a half.—*Mrs. T. J. Payne, Fayette, Mo.*

GRAHAM PUDDING.

Mix well together one half coffee-cup of molasses, one fourth cup of butter, one half cup of milk, one and one half cups of Graham flour, one egg, one half teaspoon of soda, one cup of raisins, or currants; spices to taste. Steam four hours.—*Mrs. N. O. Jones, Syracuse, N. Y.*

WOODFORD PUDDING.

Three eggs, one teacup of sugar, one half teacup of butter, one half teacup of flour, one teacup of jams, or preserves, one teaspoon of soda, dissolved in three teaspoons of sour milk; cinnamon and nutmeg, to taste. Mix all together, and bake slowly in pudding pan.— *Mrs. Rebecca Ford, Kansas City, Mo.*

A SPICED APPLE PUDDING.

Three teacupfuls of bread crumbs, three teacupfuls of apples, chopped, one teacupful of sugar, one quarter of a pound of raisins, perhaps a little citron, two tablespoonfuls of brandy, one tablespoonful of ground cinnamon, half teaspoonful of ground cloves, one teaspoonful of mace, two or three eggs, beaten separately. Cook the bread crumbs a few minutes with a pint of milk, before adding the other ingredients; add the whites of the eggs the last thing before baking. Bake half an hour, if the oven be quite hot. Serve with any sweet sauce.— *From Mrs. Henderson's Cook Book.*

TAPIOCA PUDDING.

Peel, core and cook, until quite done, six large apples; drain off the water; and beat well with one teacup of sugar. Add the tapioca, which has been in soak several hours. Stir all well together. Flavor with nutmeg, or lemon. Bake in baking dish about three-quarters of an hour. Serve with cream, or solid sauce made of sugar and butter, beaten together until light, and flavored with wine. Peaches (fresh or canned) may be substituted, and are an improvement.—*Mrs. E. Major, Fayette, Mo.*

TAPIOCA PUDDING.

Soak over night one teacupful of tapioca; add the yolks of four well-beaten eggs, one cup of sugar, one

pint of cream, and lastly, the whites, and a cup of
stoned raisins. Bake in buttered pan. Serve warm,
with brandy sauce. If eaten without sauce you must
add to the above one half cup of butter.—*Mrs. Charlie
Smith, Fayette, Mo.*

COCOANUT PUDDING.

Whites of nine eggs, one pound of pulverized sugar,
one half pound of butter, one cocoanut, grated. Cream
the butter and sugar. Add the whites of the eggs,
beaten stiff; then the cocoanut milk and cocoanut.—
Miss Eliza Payne, Nebraska City, Neb.

COCOANUT PUDDING.

One quart of milk, four eggs, one cup of grated bread
crumbs, (cake crumbs are better,) one cup of sugar, one
grated cocoanut, salt and flour. Bake an hour.—*Mrs.
W. C. Arline, Fayette, Mo.*

COCOANUT PUDDING.

One quart of milk, half a cocoanut, grated, four eggs,
a little salt and sugar, to taste; bake in a quick oven,
about thirty minutes. Serve with a sauce.

MOUNTAIN DEER PUDDING.

One quart of sweet milk, one half cup of sugar, four
eggs (yolks,) one half cup rolled crackers, one grated
cocoanut. Bake one half hour; take the whites of the
eggs and meringue the top, and bake till a delicate
brown. To be eaten cold.—*Mrs. J. H. Pearson, Fayette, Mo.*

COCOANUT PUDDING.

Three-quarters of a pound grated cocoanut, one quarter of a pound of butter, one pound of sugar, one half
pint of cream, nine eggs; stir the butter as for cake;
add the eggs, well beaten; grate the cocoanut and stir
in, with butter and eggs. Put in the other ingredients,
and bake with, or without a crust. It requires three-

quarters of an hour for baking. Some persons grate in stale rusk, or sponge cake.—*Mrs. Dr. T. J. Smith, Fayette, Mo.*

DELMONICO PUDDING.

One quart of milk, four eggs, using the white of one only ; three tablespoonfuls of sugar, two tablespoons of corn starch, one cupful of cocoanut, a little salt. Put the milk on the fire to scald : wet the starch in cold milk ; beat the eggs and sugar, and stir all into the scalding milk ; add the cocoanut, and pour the whole into a pudding dish. Beat the three whites with three tablespoons of sugar ; flavor with vanilla ; bake a light brown. Serve with sauce.

SPONGE PUDDING.

Butter six or eight slices of sponge cake ; place them in the pudding dish : make a custard of four eggs to a quart of milk ; flavor, and sweeten to taste ; pour over the cake, and bake one half hour. The cake will swell, and fill the dish.

ORANGE PUDDING.

Take four good sized oranges, peel, seed, and cut in small pieces : add one cup of sugar, and let it stand. Into one cup of nearly boiling milk, stir two tablespoons of corn starch : mix with a little water, and the yolks of three eggs. When done, let it cool, and mix with the oranges. Make a frosting of the whites of the eggs, and half a cup of sugar ; spread over the top of the pudding. Brown in the oven.—*Mrs. J. L. Morrison, Fayette, Mo.*

CORN STARCH PUDDING.

One pint of rich milk, two tablespoonfuls of corn starch, a scant half cupful of sugar, whites of three or four eggs, a little salt, flavoring. Beat the eggs to a stiff froth. Dissolve the corn starch in a little milk. Stir the sugar into the remainder of the milk : which place on the fire. When it begins to boil add the dissolved corn starch. Stir constantly for a few moments, when it will become a smooth paste; now stir in the beaten whites of the eggs, and let it remain a little longer to cook the eggs. Flavor with vanilla; pour into a mould. This pudding is improved by adding half a cocoanut, grated. Season with whipped cream. —*Mrs. J. L. Morrison, Fayette, Mo.*

"DANDY" PUDDING.

Two quarts of milk, five eggs, one teacup of white sugar; flavor with vanilla. Dissolve the starch in one quart of milk; beat the yolks of the eggs with the sugar, until light, and add the other quart of milk; pour this into the milk and starch, which has been heated to boiling; boil until thick. Flavor after taking from the fire. When cold spread the meringue over top. Place in the oven until a light brown. Serve with cream, or sauce.—*Mrs. Martha Elliott, Estill, Mo.*

SNOW PUDDING.

Cover one third of package of gelatine with cold water; stir in a pint of boiling water; add one cup of sugar, the juice of two lemons, or a half cup of wine. When cold, and beginning to thicken, add the beaten whites of three eggs. Beat all well together, and pour into moulds. Serve with boiled custard, made with the yolks of three eggs, one pint of milk, and half cup of sugar.—*Mrs Romeo Hughes, Fayette, Mo.*

GELATINE PUDDING.

Separate the whites and yolks of four eggs; with the yolks make a boiled custard, (with a pint of milk, and sugar, to taste.) Set a third of a box of gelatine to soak a few minutes in a little cold water; then dissolve it with three-fourths of a cup of boiling water. When the custard has cooled, add the gelatine water and the whites of the eggs, beaten to a stiff froth; flavor with vanilla.

Stir all together, and put it into a mould, or moulds. It will settle into three layers, and is a very pretty pudding, tasting very much like a *Charlotte russe.* A pretty effect can be obtained by using Cox's *pink* gelatine.— *From Mrs. Henderson's Cook Book.*

ORANGE ROLEY POLEY.

Make a light pastry, as apple dumplings ; roll in oblong sheets, and lay oranges peeled, sliced, and seeded, thickly all over it ; sprinkle with white sugar : scatter over all a teaspoon or two of grated orange peel, and roll up, folding down the edges closely, to keep the syrup from running out : boil in a cloth one and one-half hours. Serve with lemon sauce.—*Buckeye Cookery.*

BROWN BETTY.

Put a layer of sweetened apple-sauce in a buttered dish : add a few lumps of butter ; then a layer of cracker crumbs, sprinkled with a little cinnamon ; then a layer of sauce, etc., making the last layer of crumbs. Bake in oven, and serve with cold, sweetened cream.— *Mrs. Fratie Knickerbocker, Fayette, Mo., 1864.*

QUEEN OF PUDDINGS.

To one pint of bread crumbs, add one quart of sweet milk, one cup of sugar, yolks of four eggs, the rind of a fresh lemon, grated fine, a piece of butter the size of a hen egg. Bake till done. Beat the four whites to a stiff froth, adding one teacupful of sugar ; stir in the juice of one lemon. When the pudding is baked, spread a layer of acid jelly over, then the meringue. Set in the oven, to brown slightly. Serve with cold cream.—*Mrs. Nannie Lay, Jefferson City, Mo.*

RICE PUDDING.

To a cup of boiled rice, while warm, add a pint of milk, in which a little corn starch has been dissolved, and boil again ; add the yolks of two eggs, beaten, with half a cup of sugar. Stir well together; and lastly, add the juice and grated rind of one lemon. Place in a dish, and bake slowly in the oven. When done, spread over the top the whites, beaten, with two tablespoons sugar, and brown in oven. A cup of raisins may be added just before baking. Serve with cream sauce.

COTTAGE PUDDING.

One cup of sweet milk, one half cup of sugar, one tablespoonful of butter, one egg, one teaspoonful (level full) of soda, two of cream of tartar. Flour to make a thick batter. Flavor with nutmeg. Serve with sauce.

SIMPLE PUDDING.

Two eggs, one cup of sugar, one cup and a half of sweet milk, two tablespoons of butter, one quart of flour, two teaspoons of baking powder. Flour to taste, —*Miss Sallie Warden, Fayette, Mo.*

VIRGINIA PUDDING.

Five eggs, reserving three whites for sauce, one pint of milk, one gill of cream, or an ounce of butter, three tablespoons of flour, a little salt. Bake one half hour. *Sauce.*—Beat three whites, with one half pound of sugar. Flavor with wine, or lemon. Pour on pudding just before serving.—*Miss Bessie Gay, Fayette, Mo.*

SAUCES FOR PUDDINGS

BUTTER SAUCE.

Three-quarters of a cup of butter, one and a half cupfuls of powdered sugar, four tablespoonfuls of boiling hot starch, made of flour or cornstarch; use wine, lemon, vanilla or any flavoring preferred; stir the butter with a fork to a light cream; add the sugar and continue to beat it for one or two minutes; just before serving, stir in with an egg-whisk, the boiling starch and flavoring.

BUTTER SAUCE WITH EGGS.

Dissolve a pint of sugar, in a little water; cream a teacup of butter, and the yolks of two eggs; then add the sugar; set on the stove to boil slowly, stirring almost constantly; use any flavoring preferred.

A PLAINER SAUCE.

One coffee cup of *clarified brown sugar;* a lump of butter, size of an egg, one level tablespoon of flour, (dissolved in a little cold water); mix well together; then stir in a coffee-cup of boiling water; let boil till the consistency of cream; flavor with either nutmeg or lemon.

WINE SAUCE.

Beat a cup of butter until creamy, then gradually beat into it, two cups of powdered sugar; add a gill of *sherry* by spoonfuls; beat the mixture until it becomes a smooth, light froth; then set the bowl in a basin of boiling water, and stir for a minute and a half; have your sauce-bowl heated by means of boiling water; when the sauce is finished, empty the bowl of water, and put the sauce into it; grate nutmeg over the sauce and send to the table hot.

73

FOAM SAUCE.

Beat up as for hard sauce; white sugar with butter, until very light in the proportion of half a cup of butter to one cup of sugar; flavor with essence of lemons or bitter almonds: fifteen minutes before serving, set the bowl in a pan of boiling water on the stove, and stir it till hot; it will raise in a white foam to the top of the bowl.

CREAM SAUCE.

One teacup powdered white sugar, scant half teacup butter, half teacup rich cream; beat butter and sugar thoroughly, add cream; stir the whole into half teacup boiling water; place on the stove for a few moments, stirring it constantly; take it off, and add flavoring.

STRAWBERRY SAUCE.

Half a cupful of butter, one cupful of sugar, the beaten white of an egg, and one cupful of strawberries (mashed), rub butter and sugar to a cream; add the beaten white of the egg, and the strawberries thoroughly mashed.

COLD CREAM SAUCE.

Beat together one cup of sugar and half cup of butter; add a cup of rich cream. Stir all to a cream, flavoring with vanilla or lemon, and place where it will get very cold before serving.

PLAIN CREAM SAUCE.

One pint of cream, three tablespoons of sugar, and half a small nutmeg grated.

WHIPPED CREAM SAUCE.

One pint of rich cream sweetened to taste and flavored with wine; skim off the top as it is whipped and place in sauce bowl, or it makes a very pretty dish to place it around the pudding.

SAUCE.

One cup of butter, two cups of light brown sugar, one cup of cream cooked together.

PIES

PASTRY.

Pastry for seven pies; three uncovered; three pints of flour, one pound of butter, and a heaping cup of lard; wash the butter in ice-water to extract the salt; set the pan in which you mix the pastry, in a pan of ice-water; mix very lightly the flour and lard and butter.—*From My Mother's Cook Book.*

PASTRY.

One pound of flour, sifted three or four times; half pound lard, one-fourth pound of butter; cut up the lard with the flour and mix it with icewater; handle as little as possible with the hands; roll thin and spread with thin slices of butter; then dredge with flour; roll up and slice in about three or four pieces; roll out again, and again; spread with butter and dredge with the flour as before; roll up and stand on end; dredge with flour; roll out thin and place in pans.—*Mrs. Dr. T. J. Smith, Fayette, Mo.*

MINCEMEAT.

Two pounds of lean, tender beef; after it is cooked and chopped, half pound of butter, one pound of suet chopped fine, three pounds of apples chopped fine, three pounds of raisins, seeded and cut, two pounds of currants, half pound citron, one pound of figs, two pounds of brown sugar, one ounce of cinnamon, half ounce of clover, half ounce of allspice, one-fourth ounce of mace, juice of four oranges, and three lemons, four nutmegs grated, one pint of good brandy, one gallon of sweet cider; mix well and keep well covered.—*Mrs. Mittie C. Burton, Fayette, Mo.*

"TEMPERANCE" MINCEMEAT.

Five pounds of meat cooked and chopped fine, two pounds of suet, four pounds raisins seeded and cut, eight oranges, juice and pulp, four pounds of apples, half pound of citron, one ounce each of cinnamon, allspice and nutmeg, two pounds of brown sugar.—*Mrs. D. O. Morris, Fayette, Mo.*

MINCEMEAT.

Two pounds of lean beef, boiled tender, and chopped fine; two pounds of sugar, two pounds of raisins seeded and cut, two pounds of apples cut fine, one pound of citron, one tablespoon of powdered cinnamon, tablespoon of powdered cloves and one of ginger, one teaspoon of grated nutmeg; mix all together and set on the stove; let simmer till well mixed; when cold, add one quart of brandy.—*Mrs. H. K. Givens, Fayette, Mo.*

MOCK MINCEMEAT.

Two cups of warm water, half cup of butter, two-thirds cup of vinegar, two cups of raisins, one cup of bread crumbs or crackers, one cup of sugar, one of molasses; spices to taste. Bake with two crusts.—*Mrs. Minnie Pile, Fayette, Mo.*

LEMON PIES.

Take three lemons, cut them up fine; two cups of molasses, one of sugar, four eggs; mix well together and make two pies, in the following manner; take deep pie pans, line the bottom with a crust; put in one-fourth of the mixture into each pan, lay on another crust; put in the rest of the mixture and cover with a crust.—*Mrs. Dr. T. J. Smith, Fayette, Mo.*

LEMON PIE.

Six eggs; one teacup of butter, two of sugar, teaspoon level full of "citric acid," dissolved in a little hot water, tablespoon of extract of lemon; beat the yolks of eggs and sugar together until light ; add butter, then extract and acid, and lastly the whites beaten to a stiff froth. Line pans with pastry and bake before putting in the filling.—*Mrs. S. C. Major, Fayette, Mo.*

LEMON PIE.

Two lemons, two cups of sugar, two cups of water, two tablespoons of flour, four eggs, half cup of butter ; add all together and beat well ; grate the outside of the lemon peel in with the other ingredients; reserve the whites and beat to a stiff froth, adding nearly a cup of sugar; put over the pies when done, and brown lightly. —*Mattie Frazier, Fayette, Mo.*

LEMON PIE.

Put three large lemons in the oven and heat them; squeeze out the juice; boil the rind in half pint of water; then add juice and water to the following mixture : two cups of sugar, one tablespoon of cornstarch, dissolved in milk ; one of butter, yolks of six eggs; bake in crust ; beat the whites with half cup of sugar; spread over pies and brown slightly. This quantity makes two pies.—*Mrs. D. O. Morris, Fayette, Mo.*

LEMON PIE.

Six eggs; leaving out the whites of three ; one and a half cups of sugar, juice of two lemons, one tablespoon of butter, warmed till soft, but not oily; beat three whites, with half teacup of sugar for meringue.—*Mrs. Wm. Turner, Glasgow, Mo.*

LEMON PIE.

The yolks of three eggs ; one cup of sugar, half cup of milk, one teaspoon of cornstarch, grated rind and juice of one lemon ; juice put in last ; meringue—whites of three eggs and three tablespoons of sugar.—*Mrs. J. A. J. Rooker, Fayette, Mo.*

LEMON PIE.

Five eggs, one and a half cups of sugar, four table-spoons of flour, one teaspoon of "citric acid," dissolved in a little warm water; tablespoon of lemon extract; to three whites of eggs beaten to a stiff froth, add one tea-cup of sugar; place on the top of pies, and brown slightly.—*Mrs. Solon Smith, Fayette, Mo.*

TRANSPARENT PIE.

Two tablespoons of butter, four of sugar, one of flour; cream the butter and sugar, and add the yolks of four eggs; then the flour; teaspoon of lemon extract; line pans with pastry and bake; then pour in the mixture; when done, cover with meringue, made of the four whites, adding a tablespoon of sugar to each egg. Re-place in the oven and brown slightly.—*Mrs. George Holley, Armstrong, Mo.*

CHESS PIE.

Five eggs, three-fourths of a cup of butter, one cup of sugar; beat the yolks and sugar together until very light; add the butter after it has been creamed; flavor with vanilla; when done, cover with meringue, which should be a delicate brown.—*Mrs. Romeo Hughes, Howard county, Mo.*

CREAM PIE.

Four eggs, one teacup of sugar, one pint of cream, half cup of flour; beat the eggs and sugar together until very light, then add the flour; place the pan in which you boil the milk, in a pan of boiling water; when the cream comes to a boil, pour it over the mix-ture, stirring all the while, to prevent scorching; cook this till it is the consistency of custard; when cool, flavor with vanilla; have two pans lined with pastry; bake and fill with the custard. If meringue is used, the whites of four extra eggs are required.—*Mrs. Rowena W. Woods, Fayette Mo.*

A NICE FILLING FOR PIE.

Take prunes enough for one pie; stew and stone them; sweeten to taste; add the whites of two eggs beaten stiff, beat with prunes until well mixed; bake with two crusts; or if you have rich cream, whip it and use in place of top crust.

MOLASSES PIE.

Two cups of molasses, one cup of sugar, three cups of water, one cup of flour, one-third cup of vinegar; mix together well, and let come to a boil; let it cool, and flavor to taste; add one tablespoon of butter. This makes two pies.—*Mrs. Lanford Cook, Fayette, Mo.*

APPLE CUSTARD PIE.

Three cups of stewed apples; nearly a cup of white sugar, six eggs, one quart of milk; beat the eggs until light and mix with the apples; season with nutmeg; then stir in gradually the milk, lastly add the whites; use only one crust.—*Mrs. W. F. Potts, Fayette, Mo.*

APPLE CUSTARD PIE.

Prepare apples as you would for apple-sauce; sweeten to taste; add two eggs well beaten, and one cup of milk, teaspoon of melted butter; flavor with nutmeg; bake in one crust; the whites may be left out for frosting, if preferred.—*Mrs. Louisa Sebree, Howard county, Mo.*

GREEN APPLE PIE.

Stew the apples and run through a colander; sweeten to taste and flavor with nutmeg. Bake with two crusts.

BAKED APPLE DUMPLINGS.

Peel and core six acid apples; fill the holes with sugar and butter; have ready a nice short crust; roll in small round pieces; enclose the apples in them; place the dumplings in a deep pan (not crowding them) pour over them one pint of sugar and piece of butter

(half teacupful) and warm water enough to nearly
cover them; bake nearly an hour, or until the apples
are cooked and the dumplings are brown (a light
brown); if the water cooks down too low, fill up with
boiling water. They are very nice without any addi-
tional sauce, but some prefer a sauce of butter and
sugar beaten until light; cream butter, before mixing
with sugar.—*Mrs. John Farrington, Howard county
Mo.*

BAKED APPLE ROLL.

Roll a nice short crust in the form of a large square
spread over with apples chopped fine, sprinkle over
with sugar and nutmeg; roll the crust and put into a
baking pan. Then put over it sugar, pieces of butter,
and water. Bake slowly. Serve with sauce. Fruit of
any kind may be used instead of apples.

APPLE COBBLER.

Fill an earthen pudding dish two-thirds full of tart,
juicy apples, peeled, quartered, and cored, and the
quarters cut in two. Put in a cup of water and sprinkle
with sugar; cover with a paste of rich cream biscuit
dough. Bake nearly one hour. Serve from the dish in
which it is baked. Peach cobblers are made similarly.

DRIED APPLE PIE.

Soak the apple until soft; then stew till soft enough
to go through a colander. Season with lemon; add
sugar to taste, and one beaten egg for every two pies,
and a teaspoon of butter to each pie. Mix and bake
with two crusts.

FRIED APPLE PIE.

Make a nice pastry; roll thin about the size of a pie-
plate; put in a spoon of nice dried apples, sweetened,
and flavored with allspice; turn the crust over; cut out
with the edge of a saucer to shape it nicely; and fry in
hot lard like doughnuts.

CHERRY ROLL.

Make a nice pastry; roll it out into a thin sheet; lay the cherries thickly upon the pastry, strew sugar over them; and, commencing at the side, roll carefully till all the fruit is enclosed; pinch the edges together at the ends, and tie in a strong cotton cloth, then drop into a pot of boiling water. Serve with sauce.

TIFFEY PUDDING.

Half pound apples pared and chopped fine, yolks of five eggs, juice and grated rind of one lemon, three ounces of melted butter, quarter of a pound of sifted white sugar. Butter to be added after the other ingredients are mixed. Bake in a paste like a tart. Have ready the whites of the eggs beaten to a stiff froth and mixed with a little sifted white sugar, and flavor with lemon. When pudding is done, put the meringue on the top and brown slightly.—*Mrs. Dr. T. J. Smith, Fayette, Mo.*

PIE PLANT PIE.

Peel the stalks; cut into one-half inch pieces. Pour boiling water over and let stand till cold; sweeten well, and add several pieces of orange peel. Boil until done. Bake with two crusts.

STRAWBERRY CREAM PIE.

Line a dish with pastry, and fill with fresh strawberries made very sweet with powdered sugar; cover with pastry, but do not pinch down at the edges. When done, lift the top crust, pour over the berries the following, after it is perfectly cold. One small cup of milk (or part cream) heated to boiling, whites of two eggs, beaten and stirred lightly in the boiling milk, one tablespoon of white sugar, half a teaspoon of corn starch wet with milk; stir all together and cook three minutes. Replace the top crust, and sprinkle sugar over the top before serving.—*Mrs. H. K. Hinde, Howard College, Fayette, Mo.*

IRISH POTATO PIE.

Four eggs well beaten, two cups of sugar, two large potatoes boiled and well beaten, half cup of rich cream, piece of butter size of a walnut, flavor with nutmeg and brandy. This makes two pies.—*Helen Georgie Carson, Fayette, Mo.*

IRISH POTATO PIE.

Two good sized potatoes, boiled and well beaten; butter size of a walnut; half cup of cream, and half cup of sweet milk; yolks of two eggs, good half cup of sugar; flavor with nutmeg and one tablespoon of brandy. This makes one pie. For meringue use the whites of the eggs and one heaping tablespoon of sugar to each egg. —*Mrs. Margaret Unruh, Fayette, Mo.*

SWEET POTATO PIE.

One pound nearly of sweet potatoes, the firm yellow ones are best; half cup of butter, fourth cup of white sugar; one tablespoon of cinnamon; one teaspoonful nutmeg; four eggs, whites and yolks beaten separately, one lemon, juice and grated rind, and wine glass of brandy. Boil the potatoes and mash them; cream the butter and sugar; add the yolks, the spices and lemon; beat the potatoes in by degrees and until light, then the brandy and stir in the whites. Bake in dishes lined with good pastry, without cover.

PUMPKIN PIE.

One quart of pumpkin (after it is stewed and strained); six eggs, the whites and yolks beaten separately; one quart of milk; one teaspoon of cinnamon, and one of nutmeg; one cup and a half of white sugar; flavor with two tablespoons of wine or brandy. Beat all well together, and bake in crust without cover.

FRUIT PUDDING.

Five eggs, one cup of butter, two cups of sugar, one cup of sweet milk, one and one half cups of fruit; any kind of fruit; damsons are best. Line your pans just as you would for custard pies.

COCOANUT PIE.

Grate one cocoanut, beat five eggs with sugar to taste, until they are quite light; then beat in your cocoanut milk with about one pint of sweet milk; then mix all together; and make pies in pans lined with pastry.— *Mrs. Dr. T. J. Smith, Fayette, Mo.*

PIE FOR DYSPEPTICS.

Four tablespoonfuls oatmeal, one pint water, two large apples, one cup of sugar, a little salt; let oatmeal stand in water a few hours till it is swelled; add apples pared and sliced, then sugar. Mix all well together; put in a buttered dish, and bake till oatmeal is done. Makes a most delicious pie, which can be eaten with safety by sick or well.—*Nannie Keyser, Fayette, Mo.*

NICE DESSERTS

RUSSIAN CREAM.

Let one quart of milk boil; then add the yolks of four eggs and a cup of sugar beaten together (as if for custard): take this off the stove and immediately add the well beaten whites with four tablespoonfuls of sugar, stirring rapidly a few moments; then add a box of Cox's gelatine dissolved in a pint of warm water, and a tablespoonful vanilla.—*Mrs. R. C. Clark, Fayette, Mo.*

VELVET CREAM.

One box of gelatine, well dissolved; whites of three eggs; one quart of cream, sweetened, and flavored with sherry wine to suit taste. The gelatine when dissolved, must be left to cool before using; stir into it the three whites; whip the cream; take off the whip and stir into the gelatine and eggs, stirring constantly till all the cream is used; pour into moulds and leave to harden; used with whipped cream.—*Mrs. Dr. C. Darby, St. Joseph, Mo.*

CHARLOTTE RUSSE.

Dissolve one ounce of gelatine in one pint of milk by boiling; beat the yolks of four eggs (sweetened) and stir them in while the milk is on the fire; when it is cooked to the consistency of custard, strain into a bowl, stirring constantly; season one-half gallon cream with wine; whip to a stiff froth and beat it in, just as the custard (which should be flavored with vanilla) begins to congeal; have ready a glass bowl lined with sponge cake; over which pour the custard.

84

SPONGE ROLL.

Four eggs; whites and yolks beaten separately ; one teacup of sugar, one of flour, one teaspoon of yeast-powder, one tablespoon of ice-water; bake in biscuit pans; when done, spread with jelly and roll while hot ; serve with wine sauce.—*Mrs. Wm. Turner, Glasgow, Mo.*

BLANC MANGE.

One quart fresh milk ; a pinch of salt, four table-spoons of cornstarch, four tablespoons of white sugar ; dissolve the cornstarch in a little of the milk, stir the sugar and salt in the remainder of the milk, place it over the fire, let it come to a boil and pour it on the dissolved starch ; place it over the fire again and boil three minutes, stirring constantly ; remove from the fire ; let it stand a moment or two, then flavor with vanilla or lemon and pour it in moulds to cool, having first dipped the moulds in cold water and let them drain a moment.

AMBROSIA.

Slice oranges or pine apples in a glass bowl ; sweeten well ; have a layer of the fruit and a layer of grated cocoanut, and so on, until the bowl is full ; grate cocoa-nut on top.

APPLE MERINGUE.

Boil tart apples after they are pared and cored ; run the pulp through a colander, and sweeten to taste; to a pint of the soft pulp, stir in lightly the whites of three eggs beaten to a stiff froth ; flavor with grated rind and juice of lemon or vanilla; serve with cream.—*Mrs. M. C. Burton, Fayette, Mo.*

APPLE FLOAT.

To one quart of apples, partially stewed and well mashed, put the whites of three eggs, well beaten, and four heaping tablespoons of loaf sugar; beat them together for fifteen minutes, and eat with rich milk and nutmeg.

HEN'S NEST.

se plain blanc mange recipe on cornstarch package; take half a dozen or a dozen egg shells and fill with the blanc mange while warm; when cold, take out of the shells and place in a glass dish; cut small strips of lemon peel and boil in a clear syrup till tender; place them around the egg-forms, and make a boiled custard and pour over all. (Very pretty and very good).—*From Mrs. Owen's Cook Book.*

ORANGE ICE.

Make a syrup of one pint of water, one and a half pounds of granulated sugar; add enough cold water to make three quarts of mixture; into this squeeze the juice and most of the pulp of six oranges and three lemons; taking care to remove all seeds; put into freezer, and when beginning to freeze, stir in whites of six eggs, well beaten.—*Mrs. L. S. Prosser, Fayette, Mo.*

PRETTY DISH.—PINEAPPLE.

Dissolve a box of gelatine in half a pint of cold water; add half a pint of boiling water; sweeten to taste; flavor with any extract you may prefer; let the gelatine come to a boil. Take three or four bananas, peel and slice them round or lengthwise; lay in a deep fruit dish; sprinkle some sugar over them; then pour the gelatine over them, let it harden. Oranges may be used in same way.

TUTTI FRUTTI.

Sweeten and flavor one gallon of rich cream, and when partly frozen, add one can of grated pine-apple, citron, raisins, a few figs, candies and fruits of all kinds, chopped finely. There should be one and one-half quarts of fruit. Freeze hard and mould. Angels' food (cake) is delicious served with this cream.—*Mrs. R. P. Williams. Fayette. Mo.*

CHOCOLATE CREAM.

One quart of cream, one pint new milk, two cups sugar, two eggs beaten very light, five tablespoonfuls chocolate rubbed smooth in a little milk; heat the milk almost to boiling, and pour by degrees in with the beaten eggs and sugar; stir in the chocolate; beat well three minutes, and return to the inner-kettle; heat until it thickens well, stirring constantly. Take from the fire and set aside to cool. Many think a little vanilla an improvement. When the custard is cold, beat in the cream and freeze.—*Miss Eliza Payne, Nebraska City, Neb.*

PEACH ICE-CREAM.

Prepare your cream as for plain ice cream; and when partly frozen, add to one gallon of the cream, about one dozen soft *fresh* peaches which have been nicely chopped and sweetened. (Delicious.)—*Mrs. J. D. Tolson, Fayette, Mo.*

BANANA CREAM.

Prepare five ripe bananas, take off the skin; pound the fruit in a mortar, with five ounces white sugar, to a pulp. Beat up half a pint of good cream to a stiff froth; add the pounded bananas, and half a glass of brandy, and the juice of one lemon; mix well together, then add half an ounce isinglass dissolved in a little boiling water, gently whip in and freeze.—*Mrs. John Morrison, Fayette, Mo.*

ICE-CREAM.

Take *rich* cream; sweeten to taste; use any flavoring you like. We prefer vanilla. When it begins to freeze, beat until very light. Remove the inside frame of the freezer, and set aside to mould. When ready to serve, set the freezer for an instant in a bucket of hot water, and turn into a boat or dish.

ORANGE ICE.

Eight oranges, one pound of sugar, one lemon, one quart and a cup of water. Make a syrup of the sugar and water: skim it well; cool; add the juice of the oranges. Boil up the rinds and strain the water into the syrup, and add the juice and rind of a lemon same way. Freeze.

STRAWBERRY ICE.

Allow a pound of sugar to a quart of berries; let stand an hour or two; put through a strainer; add an equal quantity of water, and when partly frozen, add the stiffly beaten whites of three eggs to each quart of the mixture.

PINEAPPLE ICE.

Make a syrup of one pint of water, and one and a half pounds of sugar, (granulated). When quite clear, pour it boiling hot on a can of pineapple, either grated or cut in very fine pieces; add enough cold water to make one gallon of mixture; then the juice of two lemons. Pour in freezer, and when just beginning to freeze stir in the whites of three eggs well beaten.—*Mrs. Russel Caples. Glasgow, Mo.*

PINEAPPLE ICE.

One can of grated pineapple; pour into a clean napkin and squeeze all the juice out you can, throwing the pulp away; add to juice two cups sugar, and the juice of two lemons (a teaspoonful of tartaric acid will do in place of lemons). Pour over all one quart of boiling water; after it cools, freeze; add the whites of five eggs well beaten, after it begins to freeze.—*Mrs. John Farrington, Fayette. Mo.*

LEMON ICE.

Two quarts of water; two good pints of sugar and the juice of eight large nice lemons; when almost frozen add the whites of three eggs well beaten; you may add the juice of three oranges or one pint of grated pineapple.—*Mrs. Charlie T. Smith, Fayette, Mo.*

LEMON ICE.

Three lemons to a quart of water; six teaspoonfuls of white sugar; pare the yellow peel from the lemons, unless you make to use right away, as the peel gives a bitter taste; slice and squeeze the lemons on the sugar; add a very little water and let stand fifteen minutes; then fill up with water and let stand fifteen minutes; strain and freeze as you would cream.

DELMONICO.

Yolks of six eggs, beaten very light; one large teacup of granulated sugar, stirred in the eggs; half a box of Cox's gelatine dissolved in half a teacup warm water; steep one-fourth of a vanilla bean in half pint cream (do not let boil.) Then add the gelatine; then beat with the eggs; whip one quart of cream, stir all together, and pour in the freezer; freeze quickly, for the gelatine is apt to congeal before it freezes. 'Tis best to prepare the freezer before you get the ingredients ready. This quantity makes one gallon. You can use extract of vanilla.—*Mrs. Bettie Tutt Dunaway, Oswego, Kansas*.

PINEAPPLE ICE.

Take one quart can of pineapple, (grated,) add one cup of sugar, and the juice of two lemons; then pour over it one quart of boiling water, let it cool; then put it into freeze. When it begins to freeze, then add the whites of three eggs, beaten to a stiff froth.—*Mrs. E. W. Bedford, Fayette, Mo.*

PINEAPPLE SHERBET.

One can of pineapple chopped fine; three lemons, using juice and pulp; sweeten to taste; pour over this a quart of boiling water and let it soak over night or several hours; when it begins to freeze, stir in the whites of five eggs, that have been well beaten to a stiff froth.—*Mattie Frazier, Fayette, Mo.*

PINEAPPLE SHERBET.

One pineapple, (or can,) one pint of sugar, one pint of water, one tablespoonful of gelatine; add the juice to the water and sugar; dissolve the gelatine two hours in cold water enough to cover it, a half cup boiling water to be added, stir altogether and put on ice.—*Mrs. I. P. Ryland, Tascosa. Texas.*

PINEAPPLE JELLY.

Pour the juice off of two cans of pineapple, having as much as a pint of juice: take the pineapple after getting the juice all out, and put a pint and a half of water and a little sugar over it, and boil to get the flavor all out; soak half a box of gelatine in a pint of water, until it is well dissolved; then add it to the boiled pineapple; then the sweetened juice; strain it and set aside to congeal. Serve with whipped cream.—*Mary Jackson, Fayette, Mo*

PINEAPPLE GELATINE.

Pour over one box of Cox's gelatine, one pint of cold water and let it stand several hours; flavor with one teacup of white sugar and half teaspoon of citric acid; pour over this one pint of boiling water and add one pint of grated pineapple.

WINE JELLY.

Pour over one ounce of gelatine, a pint of cold water; let it stand three-fourths of an hour; then add two pints of boiling water, two pounds of crushed sugar, juice of two lemons (lemon extract and citric acid can be used if you can't get lemons); half pint Madeira wine, and a wine glass of brandy; strain in a mould; cold water should be poured in the mould and emptied just before using; it hardens much quicker on ice, or the coolest place you can find: dip the moulds in warm water just a minute before taking out the jelly.—*Mrs. S. C. Major, Fayette, Mo.*

LEMON FOAM.

Beat the yolks of six eggs, with one cup of sugar; one cup of milk; dissolve one-third box of gelatine in a little warm water; let the mixture boil, then add the juice of three large lemons and cook until it begins to jelly; pour in a mould and set in a cool place or on ice for an hour; beat the whites of six eggs with half a cup of powdered sugar and pour over the top.—*Ada B. Beck, Fayette, Mo.*

BOILED CUSTARD.

Set a tin vessel containing half gallon of sweet milk in a pot of boiling water; beat the yolks of ten eggs, with one tablespoon of flour; three spoonfuls of flour with cold milk; strain this in the milk as soon as it boils, stirring constantly; sweeten to taste and flavor with vanilla; whip the whites of five eggs to a stiff froth; cook by pouring boiling water over them; lay on custard after taking up.—*Mrs. H. K. Givens, Fayette, Mo.*

❋CAKES❋

In making cake it is quite necessary that the materials be of the best quality. Sweet butter, fresh eggs and good flour are the first requisites. Never allow the butter to oil : put it in an earthen dish and add your sugar; beat them to a cream, add the yolks of eggs well beaten, then the milk, and lastly the beaten whites of the eggs and flour. Spices and liquors may be added after the yolks of the eggs are put in, and the fruit put in with the flour.

For small cakes the oven should be pretty hot; for larger cakes a moderate one. To ascertain if a large cake is sufficiently baked, pierce it with a broom straw or knitting needle, if done, the straw will come out free from dough; if not, the dough will adhere to it. To prevent the cake browning too soon, have a paste-board with a few holes made in it (with a fork), lay on the top of the pan. Newspaper will not answer, being too light and inflammable. If it is necessary to turn or move the cake in the oven, do it very gently. If the oven is too hot, do not leave the door open, but lift one of the stove lids off a little way, for a short time. Never put the cake away until cold.

ICING BOILED.

One pound of the nicest white sugar, crushed or crystalized, *not powdered*. Four very large spoonfuls of water. I use a large kitchen spoon. Boil until the water is all out. Then pour slowly on the whites of

92

four eggs that have been beaten to a stiff froth. Flavor
with extract of lemon or almond if you prefer. Add a
drop of blueing water; and if you wish the icing to dry
quickly a little pulverized citric acid.

If cake is well dredged with flour after baking, and
then carefully wiped before the icing is put on, it will
not run, and can be spread more smoothly. The cake
after being iced should be set in a cool, dry place to dry.
Mrs. Dr. T. J. Smith, Fayette, Mo.

ICING COLD.

Beat whites of two eggs to a stiff froth ; add gradually
half a pound of best pulverized sugar ; beat well for at
least half an hour; flavor with lemon juice, (some add
tartaric acid, as both whiten the icing). To color a
delicate pink, use strawberry, currant or cranberry ;
the grated peel of an orange or lemon, moistened with
the juice and strained through a thin cloth, will give it
a handsome yellow. This amount will frost one large
cake.—*Mrs. H. A. Norris.*

CHOCOLATE ICING.

One teacup of grated chocolate, two cups of white
sugar, half a cup of sweet milk. Boil until it ropes :
then beat until cool the whipped whites of four eggs
into it.—*Mrs. R. P. Williams, Fayette, Mo.*

ICING WITHOUT EGGS.

To one heaping teaspoonful of corn starch, with just
enough cold water to dissolve it, add a little hot water,
and cook in a basin set in hot water, till very thick.
Stir in two and two-third cups of pulverized sugar, while
the starch is hot ; flavor to taste, and spread on cake
while it is hot. This will never crumble in cutting.—
Mrs. J. H. Finks, Salisbury, Mo.

FRUIT CAKE.

One and a half pounds of flour, the same of butter, and the same of sugar. One dozen eggs, two pounds of best raisins, the same of currants and citron. Sprinkle all well with flour. Two nutmegs, two tablespoonfuls of powdered mace, cinnamon and cloves. One wine glass of brandy; half a wine glass of rose water; citron put in last. This makes two large cakes.—*Mrs. H. A. Norris, Fayette, Mo.*

FRUIT CAKE.

One pound of sugar; one pound of butter; one pound of flour; twelve eggs; three pounds of raisins; one pound of citron; three nutmegs: two tablespoonfuls of powdered cinnamon: dessertspoonful of mace; a small teaspoonful of cloves: two wine glasses of French brandy: one of claret.—*Helen Georgie Carson. Fayette. Mo.*

FRUIT OR BLACK CAKE.

Twelve eggs, one pound of sugar, one pound of butter, one pound of flour, four pounds of raisins, two pounds of citron, heaping tablespoonful of cinnamon, half a teaspoon of cloves, dessertspoon of allspice, three nutmegs, teaspoon of mace. All these spices mixed in a large goblet of whiskey. The last thing put in a teaspoon of soda mixed in a half a teacup of cream.

Rub the butter and sugar together: then add the yolks of the eggs, part of the flour, and the whites of the eggs well beaten; then add the remainder of the flour, and the whiskey with spices. Mix all thoroughly together; cover the bottom and sides of cake pan with white paper, well buttered. The fruit well dredged with flour must be added just before pouring into the pan. Bake four hours.—*Mrs. I. P. Hockaday, Columbia, Mo.*

WHITE FRUIT CAKE.

One pound of flour, one pound of sugar, half pound of butter, whites of ten eggs, one teacup of cream, two teaspoons of baking powder, mixed well in the flour. Cream butter and sugar together; then add the cream. After beating the eggs to a stiff froth, add them alternately with the flour to the above mixture. Lastly add two pounds of raisins, and half pound of citron, well dredged with flour.—*Mrs. R. C. Clark, Fayette, Mo.*

WHITE FRUIT CAKE.

Whites of twelve eggs, three cups of pulverized sugar, five cups of flour, one of butter, one of sweet cream, one teaspoonful of soda, and two of cream tartar, or three teaspoons of baking powder. Flavor with vanilla, or what you like; add one pound of sweet and two ounces of bitter almonds blanched; one pound of citron cut fine; one grated cocoanut; beat the almonds in a mortar with a little rose water. Flour all the fruits well with a small portion allotted to the recipe. Bake slowly.—*Mrs. J. L. Morrison, Fayette, Mo.*

SPICE CAKE.

Two cups of brown sugar, yolks of seven eggs, one cup of molasses, one of butter, one of sweet milk, four of flour, tablespoonful each of cinnamon, cloves, nutmeg and baking powder.

Whites of seven eggs, two cups of sugar, one of butter, one of milk, one teaspoonful of baking powder, and three cups of flour. Mix alternately with the above.— *Mrs. Carrie Morrison, Fayette, Mo.*

HICKORY NUT CAKE.

Three cups of flour, two of sugar, one of milk, two eggs, two tablespoons of butter, one large spoon of baking powder, one pint of hickory nuts cut fine, flavor with vanilla or bitter almonds.—*Mrs. J. L. Morrison. Fayette, Mo.*

PRINCE OF WALES CAKE.

The whites of seven eggs, two cups of sugar, one cup
of butter, one of sour cream, four cups of flour, half
teaspoonful of soda, flavor with lemon. The yolks of
seven eggs. two cups of brown sugar, one cup of butter,
one of malasses, one of sour cream, five of flour. three
tablespoonfuls of cinnamon. one of spice, one nutmeg,
half a teaspoonful of soda, and one of whiskey. The
white part marbled with the dark.—*Mrs. Cæsar
Ferguson. Fayette, Mo.*

POUND CAKE.

One pound of flour, one of sugar, three-fourths of a
pound of butter, eight eggs. Cream the butter, and
then add the sugar: stir until very light; then break
in two eggs, and sift in a handful of flour. Mix well,
then put in two more eggs. and more flour. so on until
all are used. Flavor with rose water. Two teaspoonfuls baking powder in the flour.—*Mrs. A. J. Herndon,
Fayette. Mo.*

WHITE CAKE.

Whites of twelve eggs. one pound of sugar. three-
quarters of a pound of butter, two pints of flour. sifted
twice. one teaspoonful of baking powder. Flavor with
lemon. Cream the butter and sugar together, until *very*
light; then add the whites of eggs, beaten to a stiff
froth; after these are well mixed, add flour with the
baking powder.—*Mrs. J. H. Crump. Fayette, Mo.*

WHITE CAKE.

One pound of flour, one pound of sugar, one half
pound of butter, the whites of twelve eggs, three tablespoons of cream, one and a half teaspoons of Price's
baking powder.—*Mrs. Nettie Gannett, Fayette, Mo.*

WHITE CAKE.

One pound of sugar, one pound of flour, three-fourths of a pound of butter, the whites of sixteen eggs, one teaspoon of Price's baking powder.—*Helen Georgie Carson, Fayette, Mo.*

WHITE CAKE.

Four cups of white sugar, whites only of sixteen eggs, one even cup of butter, half cup of sweet milk, one teaspoonful baking powder, five even cups of flour, sifted five times; cream butter and sugar, add a little of the whites, which must be well beaten; then add the flour, then milk, after stirring well, add the baking powder, which must be sifted lightly into the batter; flavor with almond and use cut-loaf sugar.—*Mrs. Lucy A. Boone, Jefferson City, Mo.*

GOLD CAKE.

Yolks only of sixteen eggs, two even cups of sugar, one and a half cups of butter, one cup of sweet milk, four even cups of flour, two teaspoons of baking powder. Cream butter, beat yolks lightly with sugar, add eggs; beat until light; add flour and powder, then milk; put paper in pans and grease well. The two recipes make four cakes.

CHOICE FIG CAKE.

A large cup of butter, two and a half of sugar, one of sweet milk, three pints of flour, with three teaspoons baking powder, whites of sixteen eggs; one pound and a quarter of figs well floured and cut in strips like citron; no flavoring.—*"Buckeye Cookery."*

WHITE TEA CAKE.

The whites of four eggs, two cups of sugar, one cup of butter, one cup of sweet milk, four cups of flour, one teaspoonful of baking powder, sifted in the flour; flavor as you please.—*Mrs. Leland Wright, Boonville, Mo.*

SILVER BUNN CAKE.

One good pound of flour, one good pound of sifted white sugar, one-half a pound of butter, whites of ten eggs, one teacup of cream, two small teaspoonfuls of cream of tartar, one of soda; stir the butter into the sugar, put soda into milk, add it to butter and sugar after it is well mixed; put cream of tartar into the flour. After beating the whites of the eggs to a stiff froth, add them alternately with the flour, to the above mixture; flavor as you please. This is a never failing receipt.--*Mrs. Dr. T. J. Smith, Fayette, Mo.*

WHITE CAKE.

Whites of twelve eggs; three cups even full of sugar, five cups of flour, one of butter, one of sweet cream, two teaspoonfuls of baking powder.—*Mrs. Dr. U. S. Wright, Fayette, Mo.*

WHITE CAKE.

Three cups of sugar, one cup of butter, one cup of cream, five cups of flour, three teaspoons of baking powder, whites of twelve eggs.—*Mrs. John Ricketts, Fayette, Mo.*

ANGELS' FOOD.

Whites of eleven eggs; one and a half tumbler sifted, granulated sugar, one tumbler sifted flour, one teaspoonful of vanilla, one teaspoon cream of tartar; sift flour four times, then add the cream of tartar and sift again, but measure before putting in the cream of tartar; sift the sugar and measure it; to the eggs add the sugar lightly, then the flour, then vanilla, beating constantly till put in the pan. Bake forty minutes in moderate oven, on a pan that has never been greased. The tumblers must hold two and one-fourth gills.—*Mrs. Sides, St. Louis, Mo.*

WHITE CAKE.

Whites of six eggs; one and one-fourth cups of sugar, three-fourths cup of butter, (light) two cups of flour, one teaspoonful of yeastpowder; flavor with lemon extract: cream butter well and mix flour with it; beat whites to a stiff froth, and add sugar gradually; add sugar and whites to flour and butter.—*Mrs. Nannie Lay, Jefferson City, Mo.*

DOLLY VARDEN CAKE.

One cup of white sugar, half a cup of butter, whites of three eggs, one small cup of milk, flour enough to make it the consistency of cup cake; two teaspoonfuls of Price's baking powder, one teaspoonful almond flavoring. Bake in square tin pans. Icing: Yolks of three eggs, one teaspoonful pulverized starch, whipped into the eggs thoroughly; add pulverized sugar till it is as stiff as icing; one teaspoon lemon extract; spread smoothly on cake and put it in a cool place.—*Mrs. I. H. Rearson, Fayette, Mo.*

SPONGE CAKE.

Seven eggs; one pint of sugar, one of flour; beat yolks of eggs and sugar together till very light, then add the whites of eggs, then stir in flour very lightly; flavor with teaspoon of vanilla or lemon extract.—*Mrs. E. Major, Fayette, Mo.*

SPONGE CAKE.

Nine eggs; one pound of sugar, nine ounces of flour, juice of one lemon.—*Miss Jessie Payne.*

DRIED APPLE CAKE.

One cup of dried apples, one of molasses, one of sugar, two and a half of flour, one-third cup of butter, one egg, one teaspoon of soda, one-half cup of sour milk, one teaspoon of cloves; soak the apples over night, then simmer for two hours in the molasses; mix the ingredients, putting in the apples and molasses last; bake in a cake mould.—*Mrs. Dr. J. J. Watts, Fayette, Mo.*

LAYER CAKES

HASH CAKE.

One pound of silver bunn cake, baked in layers. Filling.—One pound of almonds blanched and pounded; one pound of pecans, powdered; half a pound of raisins, seeded; one-fourth of a pound of citron, the same of figs, juice of two oranges, juice of one lemon; make icing of whites of five eggs and one and a half pounds of sugar; chop the fruit fine, stir in two-thirds of icing, then add nuts and flavoring; spread in thick layers; use the remainder of icing outside, ornamenting the top of cake with some of the almonds reserved.—*Mrs. M. C. Burton, Fayette, Mo.*

CARAMEL CAKE.

Make layers of any nice white cake. Filling.—Three cups of coffee C. sugar, one cup of butter, one and a half cup rich cream; boil until quite thick, stirring quite frequently; then spread thickly between the layers of white cake and also over the top. It ought to boil ten or twelve minutes. After taking from the fire, pour into a bowl and beat till thick, just as you do icing.—*Mrs. J. R. Findley, St. Louis, Mo.*

RAISIN CAKE.

One teacup of butter, two of white sugar, four of flour, two teaspoonfuls of baking powder; whites of eight eggs; teacup of seeded and chopped raisins, rolled in flour, and then mixed well in the batter; flavor with lemon. Bake in jelly pans and put icing between the layers.—*Mrs. Fannie Boone, Fayette, Mo.*

BON TON CAKE.

Whites of ten eggs ; two cups of sugar, three of flour, three-fourths cup of butter, two teaspoons of Price's baking powder.

Filling.—One and a half pounds of raisins, seeded and cut fine; one pound of figs, cut fine; put into a pan and add one-half pint of good brandy, with enough water to make it soft enough for a jelly; put on the fire and mix well with your *hand* while it is warm.— *Miss Gabie Darby, Howard county, Mo.*

CHOCOLATE FILLING FOR CAKE.

Half cake of Baker's chocolate sifted, one pound of white sugar, one cup of sweet milk, one-fourth of a pound of butter, one teaspoonful of vanilla flavoring. Put the sugar, milk and butter in a small kettle and let it come to a boil, stirring it occasionally ; then add the chocolate and let it cook until thick enough to spread nicely ; add the vanilla after it is taken from fire.—*Mrs. J. W. Kilpatrick.*

LEMON BUTTER.

Dissolve one cupful of sugar in the juice of a large lemon; beat three eggs very light, mix well with the sugar; butter the size of a walnut and added to the mixture; boil till very thick, stirring constantly ; place between layers of cake flavored with lemon.—*Mrs. Wilcoxon, Fayette, Mo.*

LEMON FILLING.

One cup of sugar, one egg, one large apple grated; the inside of one lemon, half the rind grated in ; cook after mixing; let it get cold before using.—*Mrs. John L. Morrison, Fayette, Mo.*

LEMON FILLING.

Four eggs, two cups of sugar, two large lemons, put in the oven and baked until soft ; squeeze the juice into the sugar and eggs. Set the stew pan in a pan of hot

water and cook till very thick, stirring frequently.—
Miss Pensie Darby, Howard county, Mo.

ORANGE CAKE.

One pound of sugar, one pound of flour, one-half
pound of butter, one-half cup of sweet cream, whites of
ten eggs, one teaspoonful of baking powder, mixed well
with the flour; cream sugar and butter until very light,
then pour in the cream, add the flour and eggs. Bake
in layers.

Filling.—Make boiled icing of one pound of sugar
and the whites of two eggs; into this squeeze the juice
of two oranges and one lemon, using the grated rind of
one orange and one-half of the lemon; then stir in pulverized sugar until thick enough to spread nicely.—
Mrs. R. C. Clark, Fayette, Mo.

FRENCH CREAM CAKE.

One cup of sugar, and three eggs, beaten together till
very light; one and three-fourths cups of flour, two teaspoons baking powder, well mixed with the flour by
sifting several times; four tablespoonfuls of boiling
water. Bake in two cakes.

Custard or Cream.—Take nearly one pint of milk;
when nearly boiling add two tablespoonfuls of cornstarch, moistened with a little cold milk; two eggs,
nearly one cup of sugar beaten together well. While
cooking, stir constantly, till it will drop from the spoon
without running. Take from the stove; add half a cup
of butter, melted; flavor to your taste. Turn cakes out
on a moulding-board, and when cold, split with a sharp
knife, and spread the cream between.—*Nannie Keyser,
Fayette, Mo.*

CREAM CAKE.

Three eggs, one cup of sugar, three tablespoonfuls of
water, one and a half cups of flour, one heaping teaspoonful of yeast powder.

Filling.—Two eggs, one cup of sugar, one pint of sweet milk, three tablespoonfuls of flour stirred in a little cold milk. Put eggs, sugar and milk together and when at boiling point, stir in thickening, and boil until stiff enough to drop from spoon without running. Take off, and stir into this one tablespoonful of butter. Flavor with vanilla.—*Mrs. Nannie Lay, Jefferson City, Mo.*

WHITE MOUNTAIN CAKE.

Two cups of pulverized sugar, half a cup of butter, beaten to a cream; add half cup of sweet milk, two and a half cups of flour, two and a half teaspoonfuls baking powder in the flour; whites of eight eggs. Bake in jelly tins and put together with icing.

Icing.—Boil a half teacup of water, and three teacups of sugar till thick; beat the whites of three eggs well, and pour over it; beat all together till cool. Sprinkle each layer thickly with grated cocoanut, and also upon the outside icing.—*Mrs. John Henry, Jefferson City, Mo.*

CUSTARD CAKE.

Two cups of sugar, four of flour, yolks of five eggs, one cup of cold water, pinch of salt, one teaspoon of soda, two of cream of tartar.

Filling.—Two eggs, one cup of sugar, one pint of milk, one tablespoon of flour. Flavor with vanilla.—*Mrs. H. A. Norris, Fayette. Mo.*

VELVET SPONGE CAKE.

Two cups of sugar, six eggs, (leaving out the whites of three,) one cup of boiling water, two and a half cups of flour, one tablespoon of baking powder in the flour. Beat the yolks a little; add the sugar, and beat fifteen minutes; add the three beaten whites, and the cup of boiling water, just before the flour; teaspoon of lemon extract, and bake in three layers, putting between them icing made by adding to the three whites of eggs, beaten to a stiff froth ; six dessertspoons of pulverized sugar to each egg. Flavor with lemon.—*Mrs. W. C. Arline, Fayette, Mo.*

CHOCOLATE CAKE.

The whites of eight eggs, two cups of sugar, one cup of butter, three full cups of flour, one of sweet milk, three teaspoons of baking powder. Beat the butter to a cream ; stir in the sugar; beat until light; add the milk; then the flour, and beat in whites. When well-beaten, divide into equal parts ; into half grate a cake of sweet chocolate. Bake in layers, spread with custard, and alternate the white and dark cakes.

Filling.—To one pint of milk add a tablespoonful of butter; when come to a boiling heat, stir in two eggs beaten with one cup of sugar ; add two teaspoons corn-starch dissolved in a little milk.—*Mrs. W. T. Bowling, Fayette, Mo.*

ICE-CREAM CAKE.

One cup of sugar; two and a half cups of flour; whites of four eggs, beaten to a stiff froth : half a cup of butter, two-thirds cup of sweet milk ; two teaspoons baking powder. Bake in jelly tins.

Filling.—Dissolve one cup of sugar in water, boil till brittle ; add the whites of two eggs beaten well; beat till cold ; then teaspoon of tartaric acid, place between cakes.—*Mrs. L. N. Jackson, Monroe City, Mo.*

LEMON JELLY CAKE.

One cup of butter, three of sugar, five of flour, one of sweet milk, two teaspoons of baking powder, whites of eight eggs. Bake in jelly cake pans.

Filling.—Yolks of eight eggs, one cup of butter, one and a half cups of sugar, three tablespoons of flour, one-half cup of water, juice of two lemons, and grated peel of one. Boil this until thick and place while warm between the cake.—*Mrs. Dr. J. J. Watts, Fayette, Mo.*

RIBBON CAKE.

Two cups sugar, one cup butter, one cup of milk, four cups of flour, four eggs, one teaspoon cream of tartar, one-half teaspoon of soda. Have ready two tins alike; put one-third of the mixture in each, and bake. To the other third, add three teaspoons of molasses, one cup of currants, and citron and spices to suit the taste; and bake in a tin the same as the others. When done put a layer of the light cake, then spread with jelly; then the dark cake; jelly and the light cake on top.—*Mrs. H. K. Hinde, Howard College, Fayette, Mo.*

PRINCE OF WALES CAKE.

1. Black Part.—One cup of brown sugar, half cup butter, half cup sour milk, two cups of flour, one of chopped raisins, one teaspoon soda, one tablespoon of molasses, yolks of three eggs, one tablespoon of cinnamon, one of nutmeg, half a one of cloves.

2. White Part.—One cup of flour, one of butter, half a cup cornstarch, half a cup of sweet milk, one cup of sugar, one tablespoonful of yeast powder, whites of three eggs. Bake both in jelly tins, put together with icing.—*Mrs. Dr. T. J. Smith, Fayette, Mo.*

ALMOND CAKE.

Whites of eight eggs, two cups of sugar, one of butter, three cups of flour, one of sweet milk, three teaspoons of baking powder. Beat butter to cream; stir in the sugar; beat until light; add the milk, then the flour, beat in whites.

Filling.—One pound of sweet almonds (blanch and chop them), one cup sour cream, one cup sugar, one teaspoonful of vanilla. Beat all together and put between layers.—*Mrs. John Noland, Independence, Mo.*

PLAIN CAKES

COFFEE CAKE.

Two cups of brown sugar, one of butter, one of molasses, one of strong coffee, as prepared for the table, four eggs, one teaspoonful of soda, two of cinnamon, cloves and grated nutmeg, one pound of raisins, one of currants, four of flour. Bake slowly at first, bake two hours.— *Mrs. E. W. Bedford, Fayette, Mo.*

CUP CAKE.

One coffee-cup of sour cream, one of butter, two of sugar, four of flour, five eggs, small teaspoonful of soda. Beat the butter and sugar together until very light; then add yolks of eggs, well beaten; then the other ingredients.—*Mrs. J. D. Tolson, Fayette, Mo.*

GINGER BREAD.

. Beat a cupful of buttermilk until it is creamy, add to it two cupfuls of brown sugar, one of New Orleans molasses, one tablespoon of cinnamon, one of ginger, one nutmeg grated, add three well beaten eggs, a cupful of cream or milk, in which a teaspoonful of soda has been well dissolved. When all the ingredients have been well mixed add five cupfuls of sifted flour. Beat vigorously, then stir in a pound of currants.—*Mrs. Juliette Findlay, Lexington, Mo.*

SOFT GINGER BREAD.

One and a half teacups of brown sugar, the same of molasses, one cup of butter or lard, four cups flour (heaping), four eggs, one teacup sour cream, one teaspoonful of soda, ginger to taste.—*Mrs. George Boughner, Fayette, Mo.*

GINGER BREAD.

Half a cup of butter, the same of brown sugar, the same of molasses, one cup of sour milk, three eggs, two and a half cups of flour, one teaspoonful of soda, one and one-half teaspoonfuls of ginger, half a teaspoonful of cloves. Beat hard and long.—*Josephine Harrison, Denver, Col.*

GINGER CAKE.

One pound of flour, half a pound of sugar, three-fourths of a quart of molasses, half a teacup of sour cream, with half a teaspoon soda dissolved in cream, five eggs, half a pound of butter, heaping tablespoonful of ginger, one teaspoonful of cinnamon, one of black pepper.—*Mattie Frazier, Fayette, Mo.*

GINGER CAKE.

Two cups of New Orleans Molasses, one cup of boiling water, half a cup of melted butter, one tablespoonful ground ginger, two teaspoonfuls of baking powder. Flour to make a thin batter.—*Mrs. L. M. Findley, St. Louis, Mo.*

SOFT GINGER BREAD.

One-half pint of molasses (sugar-house is best,) one cup of sugar, white or brown ; half pound of butter, three eggs well beaten, one teaspoonful of soda in our, one tablespoonful of ginger. Make stiff as pound cake ; bake in a moderate oven.—*Mrs. Dr. T. J. Smith, Fayette, Mo.*

GINGER CAKES.

One quart of molasses, one coffee-cup of sugar, one pint sweet lard, three eggs, beaten separately, one very small cup of ginger, half a cup of cinnamon, two tablespoonfuls of soda put in flour. Flour enough to make them roll out easily. We use only half this quantity. *Mrs. J. W. Kilpatrick.*

GINGER SNAPS.

One pint of molasses one of butter, tablespoonful of ginger, teaspoonful of cloves, one of soda.   Put all over the fire together, let it come to a boil.   When nearly cool add flour enough to roll, roll thin, cut and bake.— *Mrs. Miller Reed, Fayette, Mo.*

SCOTCH CAKES.

Put three quarters of a pound of butter into one pound of sifted flour, mix in a pound of sifted white sugar and a large tablespoonful of cinnamon; mix it in a dough with three well-beaten eggs.   Roll out *very* thin, cut into round cakes and bake in a quick oven.— *Mrs. Dr. T. J. Smith, Fayette, Mo.*

❊COOKIES❊

SWEET CAKES.

Three cups of brown sugar, one of lard, one of butter, one of butter-milk, three eggs, teaspoonful of soda, five pints of flour, half a wine glass of whiskey. Flavor with nutmeg.—*Mrs. E. Major, Fayette, Mo.*

COOKIES.

One egg beaten with one cup of sugar, butter size of a goose egg, small cup of cream, (sour), one teaspoonful of soda. Lemon and nutmeg for flavoring.—*Birdie Smith, Fayette, Mo.*

SWEET CAKES.

Two cups of sugar, two eggs, four tablespoonfuls of thick sour cream, three cups of butter, one teaspoonful of soda; sufficient flour to make them roll; flavor with nutmeg. Bake in a quick oven.—*Mrs. Nellie Gannett, Fayette, Mo.*

CRULLERS.

One pound of sugar, five eggs, one-fourth of a pound of butter, one teacup of sweet cream, half teaspoon of soda, one teaspoon of cream of tartar; flour enough to roll nicely; fry in hot lard; when done sprinkle over them powdered sugar and cinnamon mixed.—*Mrs. Rowena W. Woods, Fayette, Mo.*

LEP KUCHEN.

Take one-half gallon of sorghum molasses, one-half cup each of allspice, cinnamon, cloves and ginger; two nutmegs, two pounds of raisins, one-half pound citron, three pounds of pecans, one pint of sour milk and one-half cup of soda, one quart of melted lard; add flour enough to make dough stiff enough to roll; take enough of the dough to cover your pan and roll one-fourth of an inch thick. Bake and then cut in squares, and ice while warm.—*Mrs. Klatt, Fayette, Mo.*

GERMAN COOKIES.

Two and a half pounds of honey, one and a half pounds of sugar, two and a half pounds of flour, one pound of almonds, (pounded) one and a half pounds of citron, (cut fine) half a glass of brandy, two ounces of cinnamon, half ounce of cloves, juice and pulp of two lemons (cut fine); mix well, and bake slowly; sprinkle sugar on while hot. These will keep a long time.—*Mrs. M. C. Burton, Fayette, Mo.*

DROP CAKES.

One pint and a half of flour, half pound of butter, quarter of a pound of sifted white sugar, one handful of currants, two eggs, a large pinch of soda. This recipe will make about thirty cakes. Drop them out of a tablespoon on a buttered tin, or stove pan and bake in a moderate oven. Dredge currants with flour before putting them in the mixture.—*Mrs. T. J. Payne, Fayette, Mo.*

APIE CAKES.

Yolks of eight eggs; one pound of pulverized sugar; half a pound of butter; one teaspoonful of soda, in four teaspoonfuls of sour cream; add flour enough to roll easily; sprinkle sugar and cinnamon over tops of cakes before baking.—*Mrs. Carrie Morrison, Fayette, Mo.*

LITTLE CAKES.

One coffee-cup of butter, two of sugar, two eggs, teaspoonful soda, in a *small* cup of buttermilk; nutmeg.—*Mrs. J. W. Kilpatrick.*

JUMBLES.

Four cups of sugar, two of butter, one of milk (buttermilk) one teaspoonful of soda, four eggs, one nutmeg, flour to roll very lightly; roll sugar on top with rolling-pin.—*Mrs. Mattie Frazier, Fayette, Mo.*

SMALL NUT CAKES.

Whites of six eggs, beaten to a froth, one pound of pulverized sugar, one pound of hickory nut kernels; beat eggs and sugar together for three-quarters of an hour, then add the kernels. Bake on well greased and well floured biscuit pans, in a tolerably hot oven; drop them out of a large kitchen spoon. This recipe makes seventy-five or eighty. You can use any other kind of kernels if you wish. Flour the pans after greasing.—*Mrs. J. W. Kilpatrick, Fayette, Mo.*

MACAROONS.

One pound of sugar, granulated, one pound of shelled almonds, whites of four eggs; put the almonds into hot water until the skins will slip off easily, then dry and beat them to a paste, with a little rose-water, or oil of lemon to prevent their oiling; beat the eggs till perfectly dry and light, then add the sugar and almonds. Bake in small cakes in slow oven.—*Mrs. Mamie White Chinn, Franklin, Mo.*

BOSTON CREAM CAKES.

One pint of water, one-half pound butter, three-fourths pound of flour, ten eggs; boil the butter and water together; stir in the flour when boiling; when cool, add the eggs and soda, the size of a pea; drop by the spoonful on a buttered baking pan, leaving space so that the cakes will not touch when risen. Bake in a very quick oven, about ten minutes; when cold, make an incision at the side, and fill with the following cream:

Six gills of milk, one and a half cups of flour, two cups of sugar, six eggs; beat the flour, sugar and eggs together, and stir into milk while boiling; flavor with lemon.—*Mrs. John Shaffroth, Fayette. Mo.*

DOUGHNUTS.

One-fourth of a pound of butter, one-half a pound of sugar, five eggs well beaten, one teaspoonful of soda, two of cream of tartar, half a cup of sweet milk; flour enough to make them roll out nicely; flavor as you please; roll out and cut in different shapes; fry in hot lard.—*Mrs. M. Bridges, Fayette, Mo.*

DOUGHNUTS.

To one cup of good yeast, add one pint of milk, one and a half cups of sugar, one-fourth cup (large measure) lard, saltspoon salt, a little nutmeg and cinnamon, stir in flour until stiff enough and let it rise, then add a half teaspoonful soda, dissolved in milk; mix stiff enough to roll and cut out to suit your taste. These require a little more time to cook than those without yeast. Fry in hot lard, and when done, sprinkle with powdered sugar and cinnamon.—*Mrs. Anne Shaffroth, Fayette, Mo.*

CREAM DOUGHNUTS.

Beat one cup each of sour cream and sugar and two eggs together, add a level teaspoon of soda, a little salt and flour enough to roll; fry in hot lard; flavor with nutmeg.—*Mrs. E. Major, Fayette, Mo.*

KNICKERBOCKER CRULLERS.

One cup of butter, two cups of sugar, four eggs, half teaspoon soda, little salt and nutmeg, small cup of milk; flour to make stiff; roll very thin; use cruller-cutter in making cakes about three inches square, with slits. Fry in hot lard.

SUGAR KISSES.

Whites of five eggs well beaten; add one pound of pulverized sugar, one teaspoon of lemon extract; drop on white paper, and bake about twenty minutes in a moderate oven.

SCOTCH WAFERS.

Take one pound of sugar, half a pound of butter, one pound of flour, two eggs, two teaspoonfuls of cinnamon; roll thin, and bake quickly in wafer irons.

CONFECTIONERY

GENERAL DIRECTIONS FOR CANDY MAKING.

Granulated sugar is preferable. Candy should not be stirred while boiling. Cream tartar should not be added until the syrup begins to boil. Butter should be put in when the candy is almost done. Flavors are more delicate when not boiled in the candy.

VANILLA CREAM CANDY.

Three cups of sugar, one and one-half cups of water, one-half teaspoon of cream tartar, butter size of a walnut; flavor with vanilla; boil until it begins to thread, or until the drops are somewhat brittle if dropped in cold water; pour into buttered platters, and when sufficiently cool, pull.

If chocolate flavoring is desired, grate it over the hot candy, or place some melted chocolate in it before pulling. A pretty variety may be made by pulling the vanilla and chocolate candies together a few times; thus leaving it striped.

CREAM FOR BON BONS.

Three cups of sugar, one and a half cups of water, one-half teaspoon of cream tartar; flavor with vanilla; boil until drops will almost keep their shape in water; then pour into a bowl, set in cold water; stir steadily with a silver or wooden spoon until cool enough to bear the hand; then place on a platter and knead until of even texture; if too hard, a few drops of warm water may be stirred in; if too soft, it must be boiled again.

114

This is the general foundation of Cream Bon Bons; it may be flavored with chocolate, by adding a tablespoon of melted chocolate while the syrup is hot.

TAFFY.

Two cups of brown sugar, one-half cup of butter, four tablespoons of molasses, two tablespoons of water, two tablespoons of vinegar; boil until it strings; cover the bottom of a dish with nuts, and pour the candy over, and let it harden.

BUTTER SCOTCH.

Three pounds coffee A sugar, fourth pound butter, half teaspoon cream tartar, eight drops extract of lemon; add as much cold water as will dissolve the sugar; boiling without stirring till it will easily break when dropped in cold water, and when done add the lemon; have a dripping pan well buttered and pour in one-fourth inch thick, and when partly cold, mark off in squares. If pulled when partly cold till very white, it will be like ice cream candy.

COCOANUT CARAMELS.

One pint milk, butter size of an egg, one cocoanut grated fine, three pounds of white sugar, two teaspoons lemon; boil slowly until stiff, (some then beat to a cream); pour into shallow pans, and when partly cold cut in squares.

HICKORYNUT MACAROONS.

Take meats of hickorynuts, pound fine, and add mixed ground spice and nutmeg; make frosting as for cakes; stir meats and spices in, putting in enough to make it convenient to handle; flour the hands and make the mixture into balls the size of nutmegs; lay them on buttered tins, giving room to spread. Bake.

WALNUT CANDY.

Three cups of brown sugar, one cup of cream, butter size of a walnut; boil until bubbles are large; have walnuts cut fine in dish, and pour candy over them. Beat until waxy, and cut in squares.

KISSES.

One egg, one cup sugar, one-half cup of butter, one-half cup milk, one teaspoon cream of tartar, one-half of soda, flour enough to make a stiff dough; drop on tins and sprinkle over with powdered sugar. Bake in a quick oven.

CANDY.

One pound sugar, one and a half cup water, three tablespoons rose water; boil twenty minutes, then pull.

COCOANUT CANDY.

Two teacupfuls of white sugar, one-half teacup of sweet cream, butter the size of a walnut; let it boil fifteen minutes; then stir in as much cocoanut as you think best. Flavor to taste.

COCOANUT CANDY.

One large cocoanut, one and a half pounds of coffee sugar. Wet sugar with cocoanut milk; when thoroughly dissolved, put in the grated cocoanut; boil until it ropes; stir till it begins to grain; spread on platters. If boiled too hard, add a little water, and repeat process.—*Marie Howard, Batavia, N. Y.*

PEANUT CANDY.

One cup of molasses, one cup of sugar, piece of butter the size of an egg. Boil a long time, until it will harden quickly when put in a saucer; then put in the nuts and pour in a buttered pan.

FIG. DATE AND NUT CANDY.

Take the white of one large egg, and an equal quantity of cold water; put them together in a bowl (without beating the egg), and stir in confectioners' sugar, until thick enough to knead like bread dough; then flavor as desired, and mould in any shape wished. If not stiff enough after adding flavoring, put in a little more sugar. The cream for the chocolates is made in the same way, "Bitter Almond" being the best flavoring. Grate the chocolate and put in a pan which is set over the steam of a teakettle; when melted, drop the balls of cream in it, and when they are coated take out with a fork. Put them on the bottom of a tin pan, (that is, turn the pan upside down,) and put in a cool place; a sharp, thin knife will remove them easily. The nut candy uses the same cream, mixing the nuts in it; and with the maple sugar candy, adding the grated maple sugar. Roll some of the cream balls in cinnamon. They are very nice.—*Mrs. Mamie White Chinn, Howard county, Mo.*

SUGAR CANDY.

To six cups of sugar, take three cups of soft water, six teaspoons of vinegar; stir until well dissolved before it is put on to cook. Let it cook until a little dropped in cold water will snap. Do not stir at all. When ready turn out on buttered plates, put in a cool place; it can be handled in about five minutes. Pull quickly with the fingers, not with the hands. When it is white and begins to get brittle, stretch on a mixing-board and cut in lengths. If any essence is desired, put it in as it is cooling; vanilla is best.—*Mrs. B. F. Ferguson, Fayette, Mo.*

TO SUGAR OR CRYSTALIZE POP-CORN.

Put into an iron kettle one tablespoon of butter, three tablespoons of water, one teacup of white sugar; boil until ready to candy; then throw in three quarts of corn, nicely popped; stir briskly until the candy is evenly distributed over the corn ; set the kettle from the fire, and stir until it is cooled a little, and you will have each grain crystalized with sugar. Care should be taken not to have too hot a fire, lest you scorch the corn. Nuts of any kind may be treated the same way.

SALTED PEANUTS.

Shell them; remove the skins; put them into a dripping pan, with just enough butter to make them glossy ; shake the pan frequently to make them brown evenly. When the nuts are brown, sprinkle with salt. Salted almonds are prepared the same way, except that their skins do not rub off so easily, but must be blanched by pouring boiling water over them.

⚜PICKLES⚜

—

Use pure cider vinegar for all pickles. Cook in porcelain or stone. Keep pickles in glass or stoneware. Look them over once a month. Throw in a handful of sugar to every gallon. At this time if any are soft, throw them out and pour off vinegar; scald it and pour over while hot. Keep pickles well covered with vinegar. If you use ground spices, tie them up in thin muslin bags.

CUCUMBER PICKLE.

Three gallons of vinegar, one pound of brown sugar, one pound of horseradish, one-half pound of race ginger, one pound of mustardseed (white), one ounce of mace, one ounce of nutmeg, one ounce of tumeric, one ounce of spice, two ounces of celery seed, one-half teacup of salad oil, one box ground mustard, handful of whole black pepper and cinnamon each; add onions.—*Mrs. Odon Guitar, Columbia. Mo.*

CUCUMBER PICKLE.

Two gallons of cucumbers (small). Three and a half quarts of strong apple vinegar, two pints granulated sugar, six tablespoons of ground mustard, six of white mustard, six of cloves and spice, each, four tablespoons of celery seed and tumeric, each, two tablespoons black pepper (unground). Boil vinegar with seasoning fifteen minutes, then pour over cucumbers and tie up while hot.—*Mrs. Mamie Chinn, Howard county, Mo.*

119

PEPPER MANGOES.

To twenty-four large bell peppers, add one cabbage head, and four onions, chopped fine: two ounces mustard seed, and one ounce, each, mace and allspice. Cut a slit in each pepper, take out seed, and let stand in cold water twelve hours; then place in kettle (lined with vine leaves); pour on boiling salt water, let stand two days; then repeat after four days; drain and stuff with the above ingredients; sew or tie up; place again in kettle, cover with vinegar: let come to a boil; then pack in jars and cover with cold vinegar. Nutmeg melons may be prepared in same way, with addition of small cucumbers, string beans, horseradish, etc., etc., for filling.—*Mrs. Julia A. Pearson, Fayette, Mo., 1851.*

SPANISH PICKLE.

One gallon green tomatoes, sliced; one gallon cabbage, chopped fine; one quart onions, quartered; one-half pint green pepper; one pint grated horseradish; one gill salt; let stand all night; then drain thoroughly, and add one gallon of good vinegar; one pound sugar, one ounce cloves, one ounce cinnamon, one ounce black pepper, grains; one-fourth pound each of white mustard seed and ground mustard; one-half ounce each of mace and tumeric. Boil till clear; stir well.—*Miss Sallie Warden, Fayette, Mo.*

CHOPPED TOMATO PICKLE.

Two gallons of green tomatoes, chopped fine; three quarts of good vinegar, one pint chopped onions, one pound brown sugar, five tablespoons mustard seed, two tablespoons each of salt, spice and ground pepper, one tablespoon of cloves; boil altogether; stir often; cook till thick. Excellent.—*Mrs. N. C. Eubank, Fayette, Mo.*

CABBAGE PICKLE.

Three pounds brown sugar: one-half pound each chopped onions and horseradish; one-half pound each white race ginger and white mustard seed; one-fourth pound ground cinnamon; one eighth pound mustard; one-half ounce each of mace and tumeric; one tablespoon black pepper; one-half bottle salad oil; three nutmegs; nine cabbage heads, quartered. Let cabbage stand in salt-water twenty-four hours, drain and put out to dry; when dry, place in weak vinegar, to which the half ounce tumeric has been added; let stand two or three days, pour off; pour boiling water over ginger, let stand twenty-four hours, slice thin and dry; scrape horseradish and dry. Dissolve the brown sugar in two gallons good vinegar; pour out the other things to make into paste with the salad oil. Mix altogether; cover close.—*Mrs. Theodore Woods, Fayette, Mo.*

YELLOW PICKLE.

One peck quartered cabbage; place in vessel, with layer of cabbage, one of salt; let stand all night; squeeze out, add four onions, cover with vinegar; boil one hour; then add two pounds brown sugar, two ounces black pepper, two ounces celery seed, one ounce tumeric, one-half ounce mace, four tablespoons ground mustard, one of allspice, a few pieces of ginger, a few cloves; boil another hour, use when cold.—*Mrs. Louisa A. Smith, St. Agnes' Hall, Macon county, Mo.*

CHOW-CHOW.

Two large heads of cabbage, six onions, twelve cucumbers, cut in small pieces; put in vessel with layers of salt alternately, over night; then drain thoroughly and add one gallon good vinegar; two pounds brown sugar, one of grated horseradish, one-half pound each of white mustardseed and ground mustard, four ounces of ground black pepper, one ounce each of celery seed, ground cinnamon and tumeric; set over a slow fire two hours.—*Mrs. L. A. Smith, St. Agnes' Hall, Macon county, Mo.*

CHOW-CHOW.

One large head of cabbage, twelve cucumbers, one-fourth peck green tomatoes, six onions, one-half pint grated horseradish; half pound white mustard seed; two tablespoons of celery seed; half teacup brown sugar; fourth teacup each of tumeric, cinnamon and ground pepper. Cut cabbage, cucumbers and onions in small pieces; pack in salt over night, drain thoroughly; mix all ingredients together; pour vinegar over them boiling hot, for three mornings. The third morning mix a small box of mustard with a pint of olive-oil, and add while pickle is hot, and seal.—*Mrs. John Noland, Independence, Mo.*

CHOW-CHOW.

Two gallons cucumbers, out of brine; soak two days in water; two heads of cabbage; thirty-six onions, chopped up, and soaked in weak brine over night. When these are ready drain well and dry in sun. When dried, cut cucumbers in small strips. Then take two gallons good vinegar, one box (50 cts box) Coleman's Mustard, one and one-half pounds sugar, two ounces tumeric, two ounces celery seed, two ounces white mustard seed; let come to a boil, add cucumbers and cabbage and one large bottle of salad oil. Boil five minutes, tie up tight.—*Mrs. Nettie Gannett, Fayette, Mo.*

CHOW-CHOW.

One quart large cucumbers, chopped fine and peeled; one quart small cucumbers, whole; one quart white onions; one quart green tomatoes, chopped fine; one quart green beans, broken in small pieces and cooked tender; one quart celery, cut in small pieces; one quart cauli-flower or good sized cabbage, chopped fine; six green peppers. Mix ingredients; let stand in weak salt water twenty-four hours, then scald in some water till cabbage is done, then drain well. Take one small cup of flour, one and one-half cup of white sugar, six tablespoons ground mustard, one of tumeric, one of celery, mix well; add two quarts cider vinegar, and boil till the flour is cooked; seal immediately. In measuring, a quart means after it is chopped.—*Bettie Tutt Dunanay, Oswego, Kan.*

CHILI SAUCE.

Thirty-six large size tomatoes; four large onions, chopped fine; six green peppers (seed taken out), and then chopped; one-fourth pound white mustard seed, or ground mustard; one and one-fourth pounds brown sugar; three pints cider vinegar; one ounce each, allspice and cinnamon and cloves. Peel tomatoes; cook well; strain through a colander; add two tablespoons salt and the other ingredients, and cook one hour.—*Mrs. John D. Tolson, Fayette, Mo.*

EYE-OPENER CATSUP.

To one peck of green tomatoes, add one dozen onions; cover with vinegar; boil till tender. Rub through a sieve; add spice to taste; also more vinegar; return to kettle and boil to the consistency of catsup. If preferred, two-third pepper catsup and one-third tomato catsup makes a good catsup.—*Mrs. H. A. Norris, Fayette, Mo.*

RIPE TOMATO CATSUP.

Cut up one bushel of ripe tomatoes; salt down twelve hours; boil until done; strain through a fine sieve; return to kettle and cook till thick; add two ounces each, cinnamon, allspice and cloves, three grated nutmegs, one ounce mace, one quart brandy when cold.—*Mrs. Martha Elliott, Howard County, Mo.*

TOMATO CATSUP.

One peck ripe tomatoes, skinned; boil soft; press through a colander; add one-half ounce race ginger; two tablespoons ground pepper; one spoon each, powdered allspice and cloves; boil slowly two or three hours After taking from fire, add one-third cup ground mustard put into a little of the mixture; then stir in the whole; add pint of vinegar; stir well; bottle and seal.— *Mrs. L. S. Prosser, Fayette, Mo.*

CHILI SAUCE.

To one gallon ripe tomatoes, add one quart chopped onions, five small green peppers; eight tablespoons sugar; one of ground ginger; one of cinnamon, two of salt; one teaspoon cloves; one half gallon vinegar; boil thick; seal hot.—*Mrs. N. C. Eubank, Fayette, Mo.*

GREEN TOMATO SWEET PICKLE.

Eight pounds of tomatoes, chopped fine; four pounds brown sugar; boil three hours, then add one quart good vinegar; one teaspoon each, mace, cloves and cinnamon; boil fifteen minutes; let cool; put in jars.—*Mrs. M .E. Jackson, Fayette, Mo.*

WATERMELON SWEET PICKLE.

Melon rind, two pounds, boil in clear water till tender, drain well; make a syrup of two pounds of white sugar, one quart good vinegar, one ounce cinnamon, one ounce each of mace and white ginger; boil syrup thick; pour over melon, repeat this three days, and it is ready for use.—*Mrs. John E. Ryland, Lexington, Mo.*

FIG SWEET PICKLE.

To seven pounds of figs, take four pounds of sugar; one quart of vinegar, one ounce of stick cinnamon, a little mace. (Cloves are nice but they make the pickle dark). Let the figs soak in cold water for twelve hours,

then drain off the water, and, after you have boiled the
syrup till done, then drop the figs in, and remove from
the fire at once. Let the pickle stand several days
before using.—*Miss Enna Davis, Fayette, Mo.*

PEACH SWEET PICKLE.

Peaches, one peck; scald in weak lye till outer skin
rubs off easily. Make a syrup of seven pounds of
sugar and one cup of water; drop peaches in and boil
till done to seed; take out peaches and boil syrup till
thick; add one quart of apple vinegar or brandy and
spice to taste.—*Mrs. H. A. Norris, Fayette, Mo.*

TO PICKLE PEARS. PLUMS, GRAPES AND CRAB-APPLES.

Ten pounds fruit (pare pears); four and one-half
pounds white sugar; one quart cider vinegar; one ounce
each, mace, cinnamon, cloves and race ginger. Lay
fruit in sugar over night; if plums or grapes prick them.
Next morning put all together, cook till done. Take
out fruit; boil sugar thirty minutes; pour over fruit;
seal hot.—*Mrs. M. C. Burton, Fayette, Mo.*

TO PICKLE CHERRIES.

Fill a glass jar with large ripe cherries on the stems;
fill up with best cold vinegar; do not cook.—*Mrs. M. C.
Burton, Fayette, Mo.*

❦FRUITS❧

To insure success in preserving, the fruits must be carefully selected. Care should be taken to remove all bruised or decayed parts, as they would darken the syrup. Fruit requiring to be pared should be laid in water to preserve the color after paring. The best sugar is the cheapest. The usual proportion in making preserves is a pound of sugar to a pound of fruit; but in fruits not very acid, such as peaches, apples and pears, three-quarter of a pound to a pound of fruit is sufficient. The syrup should always be boiled and skimmed before putting in the fruit. Fruit should be cooked in brass kettles or those of bell metal. Modern kettles, lined with porcelain, are much used for this purpose. Never use tin, iron or pewter spoons as skimmers, as they will injure the color of the syrup and impart a very unpleasant flavor. Glass jars are best for preserves, as the condition of the fruit can be observed more readily. They should be kept in a dark place, for the chemical action of light will affect the quality of the preserves when perfectly air-tight.

PRESERVED PEACHES.

Weigh the peaches, and allow three-quarters of a pound of sugar to every pound of fruit. After they have been pared and the stone removed, sprinkle sugar over the fruit, and let it stand over night. In the morning drain off the syrup from the fruit; add the rest of the sugar, and let that come to a boil. Put the peaches in, and let them boil until you can stick a straw through them.

126

PRESERVED PEARS.

Preserved pears are put up precisely as are peaches.
Cut in halves and remove the core: they can be more
easily pared if boiling water is poured over them, and
let stand for a while.

PRESERVED QUINCES.

Use a pound of sugar to each pound of quinces, after
paring, coring, and quartering; take half of the sugar
and make a thin syrup; boil in this a few of the quinces
at a time till all are finished. Make a rich syrup of the
remaining sugar, and pour over them.

PRESERVED APPLES.

Apples are preserved just the same as peaches, except when the fruit is added put in two or three pieces
of race-ginger and several pieces of orange peel, cut in
strips.

PRESERVED CRAB APPLES.

Wash and pick blows off, but leave stems on your
crab apples. Take as many pounds of sugar as there
are pounds of fruit; add a little water to dissolve; put
in part of fruit at a time; when the apples begin to
crack, skim out into a jar; when all are done boil syrup
a few moments, and skim; then pour over fruit, keep
dry and cool.

PRESERVED CITRON.

The citron can be pared, cored and sliced, or cut into
fancy shapes with cutters which are made for the purpose. To six pounds of citron use six pounds of sugar,
four lemons, and a quarter of a pound of ginger root.
Put the slices of lemon into a preserving kettle and boil
them for half an hour, or until they look clear in a little
clear water; then drain them; save the water, and put
the slices into another dish with a little cold water;
cover them, and let them stand over night. In the morning wrap the ginger root (bruised) in a thin muslin

cloth; boil it in three pints of clear water until the water is highly flavored, when take out the bag of ginger. Having broken up the loaf sugar, put it into the preserving kettle with the ginger water. When the sugar is all melted set it over the fire; boil and skim until no more scum rises; then put in the pieces of citron and the juice of the lemons. Boil them in the syrup till all the slices are quite transparent. Do not allow them to break; when done put them into the jars, pouring the syrup carefully over them. If one desires to imitate the West Indies ginger preserve, the slices of lemon may not be added; yet they are a pretty addition.—*From Mrs. Henderson's Cook Book.*

TOMATOE PRESERVES.

Choose little red, plump-shaped tomatoes, if red preserves are desired; and the small yellow ones for yellow preserves. Peel and prick them with a large needle; boil them slowly for half an hour in preserving syrup, with the juice of one lemon to every two pounds of tomatoes; add also a little bag of ginger root; then skim out the tomatoes; let them remain two or three hours in the sun to harden. Put the white of an egg into the syrup; boil and skim well, and pour it over the tomatoes. The old rule is a pound of sugar to a pound of fruit. I prefer three-quarters of a pound of the former to a pound of the latter. The yellow tomatoes are preferable.

GRAPE PRESERVES.

Squeeze with your fingers the pulp from each grape. Put the pulps on the fire, and boil them until they are tender; then press them through a colander, so that the seeds may be taken out; now add the skins to the pulps and juice. Put a cupful of sugar to a cupful of fruit, and boil all together until of a thick consistency. Green grape preserves are also nice. In managing the green grapes, halve them, and extract the seeds with a small knife. Put also a cup of sugar to a cup of fruit. Many prefer the green to the ripe grape preserves.

STRAWBERRY PRESERVES.

Select the berries as you would for the table. Allow one pound of sugar for each pound of berries; add to the sugar just enough water to dissolve it well; let come to a boil; then add the fruit, which must be boiled about half an hour; then lift the berries out, spread them on a dish, and, when the syrup has boiled until thick, pour over the berries. Set them in the sun as you would jelly until cold. Put in glass jars and seal.— *Mrs. Cyrus Thompson, Belleville, Ill.*

STRAWBERRY PRESERVES.

Put the berries and sugar, pound for pound, into a preserving kettle, and heat slowly till the sugar is melted; then boil rapidly for twenty minutes and seal up hot.

CANDIED FRUITS.

Boil peaches, pears, apricots, cherries, or almost any fruits dressed, in a thick syrup, made with a teacup of water to each pound of sugar, until tender. Let them remain two days in the syrup; then take them out, drain them, and sprinkle sugar over each piece separately. Dry them slowly in the sun or in an oven not too warm.

RASPBERRY JAM.

Use three-quarters of a pound of sugar to one pound of berries. Put sugar and berries in preserving kettle; stir together and mash until there is syrup enough to prevent burning. Let boil till, by taking some out on a plate to try it, no juice gathers about it. Then put away in glass jars, or stone jars are very nice.

BLACKBERRY JAM.

You make exactly as raspberry jam.

MARMALADES.

To make marmalade, very ripe fruit should be chosen. For peach, pear, green grape, pine-apple, quince or plum, allow three-quarters of a pound of sugar to a pound of fruit. If the fruit is not very juicy add a little water. Stir almost constantly; when the whole begins to look clear. and becomes thick by cooling a portion of it on a plate, it is done, and must be put into jars at once.

BRANDY PEACHES.

Use cling-stone peaches; yellow ones we like best. Peel them and cut around them to the stone, but not enough to divide them. Make a syrup with half a pound of sugar to each pound of fruit, and half a tea-cup of water for each pound of sugar; skim as it boils as long as the scum rises; then put in the peaches and boil until tender. Take them out carefully; remove the syrup from the fire, and add one-half pint of best brandy to a pound of peaches. Pour this over the peaches. Seal in glass jars.

PEACH BUTTER.

One peck of peaches, two quarts of boiled cider; reduce by boiling one gallon of sweet cider to one-half its quantity; pare and cut soft peaches, put into the preserving kettle with the cider; boil until they are reduced to a pulp, stirring constantly; if not sweet enough, add a little sugar; cover tight in jars.

APPLE JELLY.

Take juicy apples (Ramboes are best), take the stem and top off and wash them nicely; then cut up in quarters and put cold water on them, just enough to cover them; boil them soft afterward; strain them through a jelly bag; then take two pints at a time with two pounds of crushed sugar; boil twenty minutes, then do the same with the other juice, to be economical; pare and core the apples; don't strain so close but that you can, by adding a little more water, use the apples for sauce or pies.

APPLE JELLY.

Take nice green apples that will cook nicely; quarter the apples without paring; put them in a pan or kettle and cover over with water, and keep them covered; let them boil slowly until entirely done, then strain through a flannel bag; just let it drip, do not squeeze them. To a pint of juice put a pint of sugar. If the apples are not very acid, use a little citric acid.

SIBERIAN CRAB APPLE JELLY.

Crab apple, gooseberry, quince, plum and apple, are all made in the same way; some add less sugar to sweeter fruits. After having freed the fruit from all blemishes, put them in a preserving kettle with only enough clear water to keep them from burning; let them boil slowly until quite soft; then, putting them into a flannel cloth, press from them all the juice possible; strain the juice two or three times through a clean cloth, then return to a clean preserving kettle, adding a cup of sugar for every cup of juice, and the beaten white of an egg for the whole. The rule is to boil the syrup (without stirring) very rapidly for twenty minutes, not counting the minutes before it begins to boil. The surest way is to boil it until it runs a little thick upon the spoon, then let it run through the jelly bag without pressing it; put the jelly into glasses, and after it has become quite firm, cut out little papers to fit the tops, which should be dipped in the whites of eggs; press the edges against the sides of the glasses to exclude the air.

CURRANT JELLY.

Weigh the currants: do not wash them, but carefully remove leaves and whatever may adhere to them. To each pound of fruit allow half the weight of granulated or pure loaf sugar; put a few currants into a porcelain-lined kettle, and press well, so as to secure sufficient liquid to prevent burning them: add the remainder of the fruit, and boil freely for twenty minutes, stirring occasionally to prevent burning; strain through a flannel bag, into an *earthen* vessel, as the action of the acid on *tin* materially affects both color and flavor; when strained, return the liquid to the kettle without the trouble of measuring, and let it boil for a moment or so, and then add the sugar. As soon as the sugar is entirely dissolved, the jelly is done. Pour into glasses. Cut papers a little larger than the top, dip in whites of eggs; press the edges against the sides of the glasses to exclude the air.

✤CANNING✤

TO CAN TOMATOES.

They must be fresh. Pour scalding water over them to aid in removing the skins. After the tomatoes are skinned, put them into a porcelain preserving kettle; add no water to them; let them come to boiling point, or be well scalded through. The cans should be heated by filling them with boiling water, and allowing them to stand while the tomatoes are boiling. Pour out this water, fill the cans and seal while hot. Always have cans soldered if you can conveniently do so, but if you should have to use the wax, be very careful to perfectly exclude the air. There will be juice left after the tomatoes are canned. This can be seasoned and boiled down for catsup.

CANNED CORN.

To seven pounds of corn, put three pints of water; let come to a boil, then add one ounce of tartaric acid; stir it in well; let it boil hard, and can while boiling. When you go to cook for table use, pour off the water that may be with it, and add fresh water or milk, and boil it also; to each quart can add a teaspoonful of soda, salt, butter, and a little sugar.—*Mrs. H. A. Norris, Fayette, Mo.*

TO CAN CORN.

Mrs. Henderson says: "I have found in a Supreme Court decision, Mr. Winslow's receipt for canning corn, as follows:

"Fill the cans with the uncooked corn (freshly gathered) cut from the cob, and seal them hermetically;

surround them with straw to prevent them striking against each other, and put them into a boiler over the fire, with enough cold water to cover them; heat the water gradually, and when you have boiled an hour and a half puncture the tops of the cans to allow the escape of gases; then seal them immediately while they are still hot; continue to boil them for two hours and a half. In packing, the cut corn in the can, the liberated milk and juices surround the kernels, forming a liquid, in which they are cooked. This process, patented by Mr. Winslow, is by far the best one for preserving the natural flavor of green sweet corn."— *From Mrs. Henderson's Cook Book.*

TO CAN PEACHES.

Pare, halve and stone them. Put them in a preserving kettle; cover with water; add about a teacup of sugar; let them boil until peaches are clear; then take them carefully out of this water and put into cans; pour over them a rich syrup, made of granulated sugar, and just enough water to dissolve well. Have them soldered while hot.

Pears and apricots are canned in the same manner.

CANNED CHERRIES.

Stone the fruit; weigh it; and for every pound of fruit, take half a pound of sugar; after putting the fruit into the syrup, let it scald (not boil hard) for ten or fifteen minutes, and then can and seal. This method is excellent for use, with all small fruits.

FAMILY BEVERAGES

TEA.

Two things are necessary to insure good tea. First, that the water should be at the boiling point when poured on the leaves; water simply hot not answering he purpose at all. And second, that it should be served freshly made. Tea should never be boiled. So particular are the English to preserve its first aroma, that it is sometimes made on the table two or three times during a meal. In France, little silver canisters of tea are placed on the table, where it is invariably made. One teaspoonful of the leaves is a fair portion for each person. Tea is better made in an earthen tea-pot, which tea connoisseurs are particular to have. They also drink the beverage without milk, and with loaf-sugar merely.

Water at the boiling point is generally considered better for tea or coffee, and in fact, any kind of cooking which requires boiling water.—*From Mrs. Henderson's Cook Book.*

COFFEE.

One mill full of coffee. When ground, put in coffee-pot, break into it one whole egg; mix well with a little cold water: then pour on boiling water, sufficient to fill an ordinary sized pot, three parts full: set it back where it will simmer gently for fifteen minutes; then set it where it will boil briskly about five minutes. Do not allow to boil over, stir it down and add a few drops of cold water.

The best coffee is made by mixing two-thirds Java and one-third Mocha. Use, if you can, the Old Dominion coffee-pot. Serve with very thick cream.—*Mrs. Dr. T. J. Smith, Fayette, Mo.*

CHOCOLATE.

Scrape the chocolate and let it soak a little while in about a tablespoon of milk to soften it; stir until smooth; when the milk, sweetened to taste, is boiling, add it to the dissolved chocolate, a little at first, until thin, then pour altogether, and let boil just a minute; stir well, and serve immediately. Have cream whipped, sweetened and flavored with vanilla, is a great improvement: a dessert spoonful to each cup.

BLACKBERRY CORDIAL.

Make a syrup of a pound of sugar to a pint of water; boil it until it is rich and thick, and then add a pint of blackberry juice to every pound of sugar; pat half a grated nutmeg to each quart of syrup; let it boil fifteen minutes, then add one-half pint of brandy for every quart of syrup. When cold, bottle for use.—*Mrs. John Ervin, Fayette, Mo.*

BLACKBERRY CORDIAL.

To one quart of blackberry juice, add one pound white sugar, one tablespoon each of cloves, allspice, cinnamon and nutmeg. Boil altogether fifteen minutes; add one wine glass brandy or whiskey. Bottle while hot: cork and seal.—*Mrs. E. Major, Fayette, Mo.*

BLACKBERRY WINE.

Bruise the berries, and to every gallon add one quart of boiling water: let stand twenty-four hours, stirring it occasionally. Strain off the liquor into a cask, adding two pounds of sugar to a gallon of syrup; cork tight. Let stand till October, then it will be ready for use.—*Mrs. N. C. Eubank, Fayette, Mo.*

GRAPE WINE.

To twenty pounds of grapes, put four quarts of boiling water; when cool, press the juice from the grape well, then cover over and allow them to stand about three days; strain the juice from the grapes, and add ten pounds of sugar; let stand in the jar for a week; then skim and strain into a cask or bottles, and seal.— *Mrs. J. Dickerson, Fayette, Mo.*

CURRANT WINE.

To two quarts of currant juice, (after the currants are pressed) add one quart of water and three and a half pounds of sugar. Let it stand in an open jar until it stops fermenting; then draw it off carefully. Bottle and cork it securely.

❊MEDICINAL❊

CURE FOR FELON.

This remedy has never been known to fail if applied in time. Take a handful of Mayapple root, with water enough to cover ; boil until all the strength is out, then dip out the roots and boil down until it is thick like candy ; apply this candy on the affected part, and let it remain twelve hours, (or longer if necessary) this will draw it so you can easily pick it with a needle to let the corruption out. When you take the Mayapple off, apply a poltice made of white beans, to draw out the poison.—*Mrs. E. M. Woods, Fayette, Mo.*

REMEDY FOR WOUNDS.

A correspondent of the *Country Gentleman*, gives the following remedy for painful wounds. Take a pan or shovel with burning coals, and sprinkle on them common brown sugar, and hold the wounded part in the smoke : in a few minutes the pain will be allayed and recovery rapidly proceed.

REMEDY FOR BEE STINGS.

The juice of a red onion is a perfect antidote for the sting of bees, wasps, hornets, etc. The sting of the honey bee, which is always left in the wound, should first be removed.—*Mrs. Mary Gay.*

BEE STING.

The sting of a bee or wasp may be almost instantly relieved by applying lean raw meat. It is said to cure the bite of a rattlesnake, and to relieve erysipelas.

138

AN EXCELLENT SALVE.

Take a piece of wax, yellow or white, size of walnut; same of resin, and same of fresh butter (before it has been salted) and melt in a tin cup; set in a pot of water; stir until cold.

A SURE CURE FOR GRAVEL.

Take one pound of anvil dust, pound it up fine, sift it through a piece of gauze, then take half as much horseradish, scrape it fine; then put both in half gallon of strong vinegar; put in a stone jug. Shake well before using; dose teaspoonful every three or four hours.—*George Frazier, Aug. 13, 1849.*

COUGH MEDICINE.

One tumbler of good vinegar; two tumblers of white sugar, twenty grains of ipecac, a lump of resin, as large as a filbert. Let all come to a boil, when cool, add a dessert spoonful of laudanum. Dose, a teaspoonful three times a day, or oftener if the cough is troublesome.—*Mrs. Fratie Knickerbocker, Dec. 12, 1863.*

COUGH SYRUP.

Take elderberries when ripe, pick off the stems and press the juice from them; put on the fire and boil as you would for jelly; when done, strain the juice from the berries, and to each pint of juice, add a pint of sugar. Boil down to a rich syrup; when cool, add a tablespoonful of good whiskey or brandy. Dose, a teaspoonful every two or three hours.—*Mrs. Anne Shafroth.*

REMEDY FOR BURNS.

Take best castile soap; scrape fine with a knife; add water in small quantities to make a smooth paste; spread upon linen; and applied to a burn quickly relieves the pain. Turpentine applied is also good for burns.

FOR SORE THROAT.

Cut slices of salt pork or fat bacon; simmer a few moments in hot vinegar, and apply to throat as hot as possible. When this is taken off, as the throat is relieved, put around a bandage of soft flannel. A gargle of equal parts of borax and alum, dissolved in water is also excellent.

TO REMOVE DISCOLORATION FROM BRUISES.

Apply a cloth wrung out in very hot water, and renew frequently until the pain ceases.

MUSTARD PLASTER.

Mix together equal parts of mustard flour with wheat flour, and enough water or vinegar to make a moist paste of them; spread it on a piece of old muslin twice the size wanted, leaving about an inch clear on the edge, and double the other half over it. It must never raise a blister, only leave on long enough to redden the skin. After it is removed, put on a rag, spread with cold cream or lard.

CURE FOR CHAPPED HANDS.

One ounce of glycerine, one of gum camphor, one-half pound of mutton tallow. Make into a salve.

———

To keep the hands nice and smooth, use the following preparation each time they are washed. Three parts of rosewater to two parts of glycerine, well mixed, and kept in a bottle ready for use. For those who cannot use glycerine, equal parts of lard and white of egg thoroughly beaten together, and scented according to choice, is an excellent remedy for chapped or rough hands.

BEEF TEA.

Cut a pound of best lean steak in small pieces: place in glass fruit jar (a perfect one), cover tightly and set in a pot of cold water; heat gradually to boil, and continue this steadily three or four hours until the meat is like white rags, and the juice thoroughly extracted; strain from the jar as you want to use it. It is best to set kettle off stove and let cool, before removing the jar, and in this way prevent breakage. When ready to use, pour into a small saucer, heat, and season with salt and pepper.

MUTTON AND VEAL BROTH.

Boil a piece of mutton till it comes to pieces; then strain the broth and let it get cold, so that the fat will rise, which must be taken off, then warm it: and put in a little salt. Veal broth may be made in the same way, and is more delicate for sick persons.

CHICKEN BROTH.

Take the first and and second joints of a chicken; boil in one quart of water till very tender, and season with a very little salt and pepper.

SWEET CIDER SOUP.

Boil one pint of cider; add one teaspoonful of flour, dissolved in a little water; one teaspoonful of sugar; pour this over the well beaten yolk of an egg; put the beaten white on the top. This is pleasant and very strengthening.

141

RYE MUSH.

This is a nourishing and light diet for the sick, and is by some preferred to mush made of Indian meal. Four large spoonfuls of rye flour, mixed smooth in a little water, and stirred in a pint of boiling water; let boil twenty minutes, stirring frequently. Nervous persons who sleep badly, rest much better after a supper of corn or rye mush, than if they take tea or coffee.

CORN GRUEL.

Mix two spoonfuls of sifted cornmeal in some water; have a clean skillet with a pint of boiling water in it; stir it in, and when done, season it with salt to your taste, or sugar if you prefer it.

OATMEAL GRUEL.

Mix two spoonfuls of oatmeal, with as much water as will mix easily, and stir it in a pint of boiling water in a saucepan, until perfectly smooth; let it boil a few minutes; season it with sugar and nutmeg, and pour it out on a slice of bread, toasted, and cut up. If the patient should like them, you may put in a few raisins, stoned and cut up. This will keep good a day, and if nicely warmed over, is as good as when fresh.

PANADA.

Put some crackers, crusts of dry bread, or dried rusk, in a saucepan with cold water, and a few raisins; after it has boiled half an hour, put in sugar, nutmeg, and half a glass of wine, if the patient has no fever. If you have dried rusk, it is a quicker way to put the rusk in a bowl with some sugar, and pour boiling water over it. If the patient can use nothing but liquids, this makes a good drink when strained.

BOILED CUSTARD.

Beat an egg with a heaped teaspoonful of sugar; stir it into a teacupful of boiled milk, and stir till it is thick; pour it in a bowl on a slice of toast, cut up, and grate a little nutmeg over it.

EGG-NOG.

Beat the yolk of an egg with a tablespoonful of sugar, add about a tablespoonful of brandy, stirring well as it is poured in; tablespoonful of cream, a little nutmeg, and the well beaten white of the egg last.

THICKENED MILK.

Boil a pint; dissolve one teaspoonful of cornstarch in a little cold milk; add to the boiling milk, stirring constantly, until thick enough; take from the fire; sweeten and flavor with nutmeg. In boiling milk, always set your saucepan in which you boil the milk, in a pan of boiling water.

Many of the articles under "desserts" are nice for the sick. In preparing food for the sick, much care should be taken, and it should be presented in the most inviting way, always the *nicest* china and silver used.

TABLE OF WEIGHTS AND MEASURES.

4 cups wheat flour make............ ....1 pound.

3½ cups of cornmeal make...... ....1 pound.

2 large coffee-cups granulated sugar make............. ....1 pound.

2 large coffee-cups dry brown sugar make........ ....1 pound.

1½ cups firm butter pressed down, make........ ....1 pound.

2 cups raisins make....... ....1 pound.

10 eggs make....... ....1 pound.

1 white of egg makes....... ....1 ounce.

1 yolk of egg makes...... ....1 ounce.

16 ounces make... ....1 pound.

4 teaspoons make............ ....1 tablespoon.

4 tablespoons make... ....½ gill

8 tablespoons make...... ....1 gill.

2 gills make........ ....½ pint.

2 pints make...... ....1 quart.

4 quarts make...... ....1 gallon.

8 quarts make....... ....,, ...1 peck.

A cup of flour means, a cup of *unsifted* flour.

MISCELLANEOUS

RECIPE FOR HARD SOAP.

Ten pounds of soda ash, five pounds of unslacked lime, ten gallons of soft water; boil two hours; adding water as it boils down, so as to have as much water when done boiling as you had when you commenced. Let it stand over night. Drain off in a clean kettle; then add thirty pounds of clear grease, if you have it, if not, and it is trimmings, add a few pounds more. Boil one hour; let stand till cold. Cut out in bars, and let dry before putting away.

TO MIX WHITEWASH.

Pour a kettle of boiling water on a peck of unslacked lime: put in two pounds of whiting, and one-half pint salt; when all are mixed together, put in one-half ounce of Prussian blue, finely powdered; add water to make it a proper thickness to put on a wall.

WHITEWASH FOR BUILDINGS OR FENCES.

Put in a barrel one bushel of best unslacked lime; pour on it two buckets of boiling water; and when it is mixed, put in six pounds of fine whiting; fill up the barrel with water: stir it well and keep it covered from the rain; let it stand several days before you use it; then stir it up; thin it with milk as you use it, and put one-half a pint of salt to each bucketful. This makes a durable wash for a rough cast or frame house, or for fences; the salt prevents it from peeling off.

146

ECONOMICAL PAINT.

Skim milk, two quarts; fresh slacked lime, eight ounces; linseed oil, six ounces; white burgundy pitch, two ounces; Spanish white, three pounds. The lime to be slacked in water, exposed to the air, mixed in one-fourth of the milk; the oil in which the pitch is previously dissolved, to be added a little at a time; then the rest of the milk, and afterwards the Spanish white. This quantity is sufficient for twenty square yards, two coats, and the expense not more than twenty-five cents.

TO STOP CRACKS IN IRON VESSELS.

Mix wood ashes and salt into a paste with a little water; apply whether the vessels are cold or hot.

CEMENT.

Three parts ashes, three parts clay, and one sand, is said to make a cement as hard as marble, and impervious to water.

CEMENT FOR CHINA.

Take plaster of Paris and mix it with liquid gum arabic into a paste. This is said to be excellent.

TO REMOVE MILDEW.

Soak the parts of the cloth that are mildewed in two parts chloride of lime to four parts of water, for about four hours, or until the mildew has disappeared; then thoroughly rinse it in clear water.

CLEANSING FLUID.

Four ounces of ammonia, four ounces of white castile soap, two ounces of alcohol, two ounces of glycerine two ounces of ether. Cut the soap up fine; dissolve in one quart of soft water over the fire; then add four quarts of cold water. When nearly cold add the other ingredients. This will make almost eight quarts.

HAIR WASH.

Take sugar of lead, lac sulphur, of each one and a half drachms or teaspoonfuls; bay rum, one-fourth pint; glycerine, two ounces.

HAIR WASH "EUREKA."

One ounce of borax, one ounce lac sulphur, one ounce of sugar lead, two ounces of bay rum, three pints of rain water.

WASHING COMPOUND.

One-half pound of super-carbonate soda, one-half pound unslacked lime, one gallon boiling water; boil twenty minutes. Pour off the top after letting it stand to settle; then bottle. Sort your clothes, soap them, and then soak over night. In the morning wring out; soap, if more is needed, and put a teaspoonful of the fluid to a boiler of clothes; boil one-half hour. They will need but little rubbing. This does not injure the clothes.

POWDER FOR SCENT BAGS.

One ounce each of coriander seed, orris root, rose leaves, lavender flowers, and sweet calamus; one drachm of mace and allspice. Mix and put in your bags, or between the covers of your handkerchief-box lid.

TO PREVENT RUSTING.

To prevent metals from rusting, melt together three parts lard and one of resin, and apply a very thin coating. It will preserve Russia-iron stoves and grates from rusting during summer, even in damp situations. The effect is equally good in brass, copper, steel, etc.

TO POLISH TINWARE.

First rub the tin with a damp cloth; then take dry flour and rub it on with your hand; take an old newspaper and rub the flour off, and the tin will shine as

well as if half an hour had been spent in rubbing with
brick dust or powders.

TO RESTORE FURNITURE.

Make a mixture of three parts of linseed oil, and one
part spirits of turpentine; put it on with a woolen cloth,
and when dry, rub with a woolen cloth or chamois.
Good for cleaning picture frames and restoring furniture
marred or scratched. It covers the disfigured surface,
and restores wood to its original color, leaving a lustre
upon the surface.

SCOURING LIQUID FOR BRASS.

Oil of vitriol, one ounce; sweet oil, one-half gill;
pulverized rotten stone, one gill; rain water, one and
a half pints. Mix well and shake as used. Apply with
a rag, and then polish with buckskin or old woolen.

SPOTS ON VARNISHED FURNITURE

Are readily removed by rubbing them with essence of
peppermint, or spirits of camphor, and afterwards with
furniture polish or oil.

TO CLEAN SILVER.

Wash silver in very hot, clear water, wipe dry with a
soft towel, and you will have no need for any preparation.

TO REMOVE A GLASS STOPPER

From a bottle, hold a lighted match to the neck of the
bottle, and the heat will cause the neck so to expand
that the stopper will loosen.

FOR TAKING OUT GREASE SPOTS.

Gasoline is splendid for cleaning grease out of any-
thing, from a piece of point lace to a carpet. Wash
lace or silk handkerchiefs in it; rub larger things with
a sponge; but it is explosive, and so must be kept far
from the fire.

TO EXTRACT INK.

To extract ink from cotton, silk and woolen goods, saturate the spot with spirits of turpentine, and let it remain several hours; then rub it between the hands. It will crumble away without injuring either the color or texture of the article.

TO TAKE INK OUT OF LINEN

Dip the spotted part in pure tallow, melted; then wash out the tallow and the ink will disappear.

TO REMOVE TAR.

Rub well with clean lard, afterwards wash with soap and warm water. Apply this to either hands or clothing.

STOVE POLISH.

Stove lustre, when mixed with turpentine and applied in the usual manner, is blacker, more glossy, and more durable than when mixed with any other liquid. The turpentine prevents rust, and when put on an old, rusty stove will make it look as well as new.

TO WASH OIL-CLOTH.

Oil-cloth may be made to have a fresh, new appearance, by washing it every month with a solution of sweet milk, with the white of one beaten egg. Soap, in time, injures oil-cloth. A very little "boiled oil," freshens up an oil-cloth. Very little must be used, and rubbed in with a rag. Equal parts of copal varnish, I put; it gives a gloss.

SWEETENING STONE JARS.

"Having some stone jars in which lard had been placed until they became unfit for use, I made perfectly sweet by packing them full of fresh earth, and letting it remain two or three weeks. I suspect this course would be equally effective in any case of foul earthen or stoneware."

RANCID BUTTER

May be remedied by putting in a saucepan and scalding; then put in a piece of toasted bread which will absorb all the bad part of the butter; pour off carefully into a clean dish, from the dark sediment which will be found in the bottom of the saucepan.

A USEFUL DRUG.

Ammonia, or as it is generally called spirits of hartshorn, is a powerful alkali, and dissolves grease and dirt with great ease. For washing paint, put a teaspoonful in a quart of moderately hot water; dip in a flannel cloth and then wipe off the woodwork; no scrubbing will be necessary. For taking grease spots from any fabric, use the ammonia nearly pure; then lay white blotting paper over the spot; then iron it lightly. In washing lace, put about twelve drops in a pint of warm suds. To clean silver, mix two teaspoonfuls of ammonia in a quart of hot suds. Put in your silverware and wash; using an old nail brush or tooth brush for the purpose. For cleaning hair brushes, etc., simply shake the brushes up and down in a mixture of a tablespoonful of ammonia to one pint of hot water; when they are cleansed, rinse them in cold water and stand them in the wind or in a hot place to dry; and for taking out the red stains produced by the strong acids in blue and black cloths, there is nothing better than ammonia.

TO CLEAN HAIR BRUSHES.

Do not use soap, but put a tablespoon of hartshorn into the water, having it only tepid, and dip up and down until clean; then dry with the brushes down, and they will be like new ones. If you do not have ammonia. use soda ; a teaspoonful dissolved in the water will do very well.

Nails dipped in soap, will drive easily in hard wood.

Mica windows in stoves, when smoked, are readily cleaned by taking out and thoroughly washing with vinegar, a little diluted. If the black does not come off at once, let it soak a little.

White clothes may be whitened in washing, by boiling a teaspoonful of turpentine with them.

A little borax put in the water in which scarlet napkins and red bordered towels are to be washed, will prevent them from fading.

A small quantity of diluted vitriol will take stains out of marble. Wet the spots with the acid, and in a few minutes rub briskly with a soft linen cloth till they disappear.

LIST OF CONTRIBUTORS,

Mrs. W. C. Arline, Fayette.
" E. W. Bedford, Fayette.
Miss Ada B. Beck, Fayette.
Mrs. T. R. Betts, Fayette.
Judge T. R. Betts, Fayette.
Mrs. Lucy Boone, Jefferson City.
" George Boughner, Fayette.
" G. Bower, Fayette.
" W. T. Bowling, Fayette.
" M. J. Breaker, Fayette.
" M. Bridges, Fayette.
" Mittie C. Burton, Fayette.
" Russel Caples, Glasgow.
" Evelina Carson, Fayette.
Miss Helen Georgia Carson, Fayette.
Mrs. Mamie White Chinn, Franklin.
" R. C. Clark, Fayette.
" Lankford Cook, Fayette.
" Samuel Copp, St. Louis.
" J. H. Crump, Fayette.
" Dr. C. Darby, St. Joseph.
Miss Gabie Darby, Howard Co.
" Pensie Darby, Howard Co.
Miss Emma Davis, Fayette.
Mrs. J. Dickerson, Fayette.
" Bettie Tutt Dunaway, Oswego, Ks.
" Martha Elliott, Howard Co.
" John Ervin, Fayette.
" J. R. Estill, Estill.
" N. C. Eubank, Fayette.
" Fannie Everett, Fayette.
" H. Everett, Council Bluffs, Iowa.
Miss Mattie Frazier, Fayette.
Mrs. John Farrington, Howard Co.
" Cæsar Ferguson, Fayette.
" J. R. Findley, St. Louis.
" Juliette Findley, Lexington.

Mrs. L. M. Findley, St. Louis
" J. H. Finks, Salisbury.
" Lizzie Fisher, Fayette
" Rebecca Ford, Kansas City.
Miss Bessie Gay, Fayette.
Mrs. Nettie Gannett, Fayette.
" Mary Gay, Fayette.
" H. K. Givens, Fayette.
" Odon Guitar, Columbia.
Miss Josephine Harrison, Denver, Col.
Mrs. M. Hendrix, Fayette.
" John Henry, Jefferson City.
" A. J. Herndon, Fayette.
Miss Lizzette Herndon, Fayette.
Mrs. H. K. Hinde, Howard Col., Fayette.
" I. P. Hockaday, Columbia.
" George Holley, Armstrong.
Miss Marie Howard, Batavia, N. Y.
Mrs. Romeo Hughes, Fayette.
" L. N. Jackson, Monroe City.
" M. E. Jackson, Fayette.
Miss Mary Jackson, Fayette.
" Cora Jones, Syracuse, N. Y.
Mrs. N. O. Jones, Syracuse, N. Y.
" Jacob Keyser, Fayette.
Miss Jennie Keyser, Fayette.
" Nannie Keyser, Fayette.
" Nellie Keyser, Fayette.
Mrs. J. W. Kilpatrick, Fayette.
" J. Kinney, Franklin.
" J. M. Kinney, Franklin.
" Klatt, Fayette.
" Fratie Knickerbocker, Fayette.
" Nannie Lay, Jefferson City.
" Jeannette Leonard, Fayette.
" Elizabeth Major, Fayette.
" S. C. Major, Fayette.

153

Mrs. John McCrary, Huntsville.
" Joseph Memmel, Fayette.
" D. O. Morris, Fayette.
" Carrie Morrison, Fayette.
" J. L. Morrison, Fayette.
" John Morrison, Fayette.
" Mumpower, Fayette.
" John Noland, Independence.
" H. A. Norris, Fayette.
" Eliza Payne, Nebraska City, Neb.
Miss Jessie Payne, Fayette.
Mrs. T. J. Payne, Fayette.
" J. H. Pearson, Fayette.
" Julia A. Pearson, Fayette.
" M. Pile, Fayette.
" W. F. Potts, Fayette.
" I. S. Prosser, Fayette.
" Miller Reed, Fayette.
" John Ricketts, Fayette.
" W. M. Robertson, Fayette.
" J. A. J. Rooker, Fayette.
" I. P. Ryland, Tascosa, Texas.
" John E. Ryland, Lexington.
" Maria Schotte, Fayette.
" Louisa Sebree, Fayette.
" Annie Shaffroth, Fayette.
" John Shafroth, Denver, Col.
" Sides, St. Louis.
" S. P. Simpson, St. Louis.

Mrs. Charlie Smith, Fayette.
" Dr. J D. Smith, St. Joseph.
" Dr. Tom Smith, Fayette.
" Dr. T. J. Smith, Fayette.
" Louisa A. Smith, Macon Co.
" Solon Smith, Fayette.
" Wilson Smith, Fayette.
Miss Lou Smith, Fayette.
" Birdie Smith, Fayette.
Mrs. Dr. Snelson, St. Joseph.
" Cyrus Thompson, Belleville, Ill.
" W. F. Tieman, Fayette
" John Tippett, Keytesville.
" J. D. Tolson, Fayette.
" " Treat, St. Louis.
" Wm. Turner, Glasgow.
" Margaret Unrah, Fayette.
" Margaret Unruh, Fayette.
Miss Sallie Warden, Fayette.
Mrs. Dr. J. J. Watts, Fayette.
" Hampton L. Watts, Fayette.
" Wilcoxon, Fayette.
" J. F. Williams, Macon City.
" R. P. Williams, Fayette.
" E. M. Woods, Fayette.
" Rowena W. Woods, Fayette.
" Theodore Woods, Fayette.
" Leland Wright, Boonville.
" Dr. U. S. Wright, Fayette.

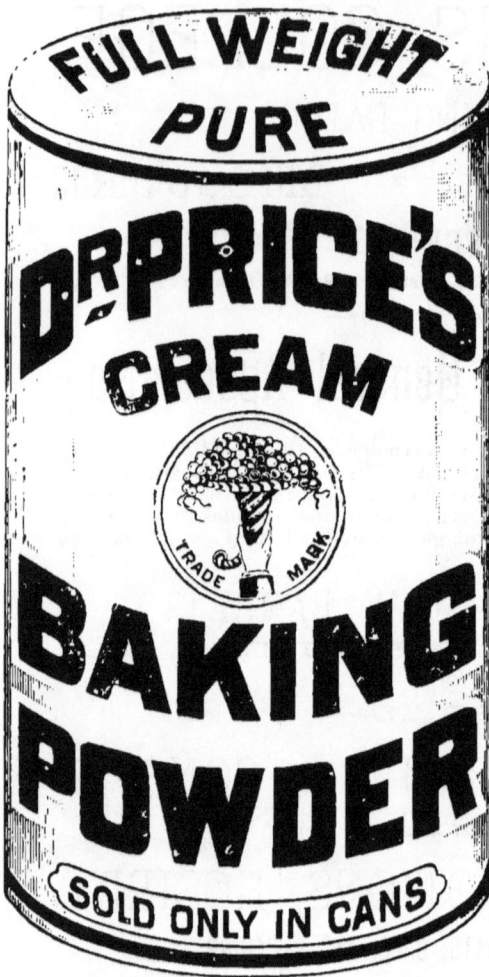

MOST PERFECT MADE.

Prepared with strict regard to Purity, Strength, and Healthfulness. Dr. Price's Baking Powder contains no Ammonia, Lime, Alum or Phosphates. Dr. Price's Extracts, Vanilla, Lemon, Orange, etc., flavor deliciously. PRICE BAKING POWDER CO. CHICAGO. ST. LOUIS.

INDEX.

157

Meats.—Continued.

Sauces for Meats.

Poultry.

Salads and Side Dishes.

Vegetables.

Puddings.—Continued.

Sauces for Puddings.

Pies.

Nice Desserts.

Confectionery.

Pickles.

Fruits.

Canning.

Family Beverages.

Medicinal.

Food for the Sick.

Miscellaneous.